T0196048

Bawdy JOKES *& Patter* SONGS

DENNY HATCH

ARCHWAY
PUBLISHING

Copyright © 2021 Denny Hatch.

All rights reserved. No part of this book may be used or reproduced by any means, graphic, electronic, or mechanical, including photocopying, recording, taping or by any information storage retrieval system without the written permission of the author except in the case of brief quotations embodied in critical articles and reviews.

Music and lyrics of recent patter songs (post1926 are most likely under copyright by the composers and lyricists. Performance permissions must be granted by the copyright holders.

Archway Publishing books may be ordered through booksellers or by contacting:

Archway Publishing
1663 Liberty Drive
Bloomington, IN 47403
www.archwaypublishing.com
844-669-3957

Because of the dynamic nature of the Internet, any web addresses or links contained in this book may have changed since publication and may no longer be valid. The views expressed in this work are solely those of the author and do not necessarily reflect the views of the publisher, and the publisher hereby disclaims any responsibility for them.

Any people depicted in stock imagery provided by Getty Images are models, and such images are being used for illustrative purposes only.
Certain stock imagery © Getty Images.

Cover Art: Stu Heinecke
Cover Design: Denny Hatch and Andrew Mays

ISBN: 978-1-6657-0917-0 (sc)
ISBN: 978-1-6657-0916-3 (e)

Library of Congress Control Number: 2021913297

Print information available on the last page.

Archway Publishing rev. date: 10/07/2021

WELCOME TO BAWDY JOKES AND PATTER SONGS

The Funniest Joke in the History of the World!

If you know a funnier joke, I'd sure like to hear it.

In 1956-58, I worked nights and weekends during college as an NBC page at New York's RCA building. My job was manning the main hall information booth and guiding audiences in and out of NBC Studios and theaters around town.

Monday evenings, four of us pages took the subway uptown to NBC's Century Theater, where a young (age thirty-two) Buddy Hackett was starring in the live sitcom *Stanley*. (Back then, all TV was live and black-and-white.) Hackett was a homely, overweight little gnome of a guy with a thick Brooklyn accent. The program was amusing, and *Stanley* lasted two seasons.

A half century later, Buddy Hackett surfaced in one of many *Tonight Show* appearances with the irrepressible Johnny Carson. He was a much older little Pillsbury Doughboy of a comic with one exception. He told—and acted out—what has to be the funniest joke in the history of the world. His schtick that night was three animal jokes, about a chicken, a cow, and a duck.

I invite you to watch the video of Buddy telling the chicken and cow jokes. Then fasten your seat belt for the duck joke.

Here's the link:

https://www.youtube.com/watch?v=aww4HT5g7ig

Note: If you are reading the print version of *Bawdy Jokes and Patter Songs* (or if the link above fails to connect), turn on your iPhone, iPad, laptop, desktop computer, or smart TV, go to the YouTube search box at the top, and enter these YouTube Key Words:

This Is Your Introduction to
Over One Hundred YouTube Video Delights!

The video of this duck joke is the first of many hours of sheer joy you will experience in what I believe to be the world's most comprehensive anthology of funny jokes (in print), plus eighty-seven English-language patter songs on YouTube performed by more than one hundred mesmerizing stage, screen, and nightclub entertainers, composers, and lyricists.

You're gonna love it. Guaranteed!

Enjoy!

With awe and thanks!

Noël Coward
Buddy Hackett
Gilbert and Sullivan
Martyn Green
Danny Kaye
Tom Lehrer
Cole Porter
Madame Spivy

All the lyricists, composers, and
performers who made this
anthology possible

Plus
Chad Hurley,
Steve Chen,
Jawed Kari,
and
the amazing video
editors at YouTube

A special thank-you to
Stu Heinecke

CONTENTS

Part 1

QUICKIE INTRO

The Genesis of This Odd Book
With 110 YouTube Performance Videos

I'm eighty-five. The past two years have not been happy for many in the United States (or the rest of the world). We've experienced lockdown, isolation from friends and family, morbid fear of the COVID-19 killer, twenty-two million jobs lost, fifty million Americans with not enough food, seventeen million starving US children, breadlines, masks that fog eyeglasses, obliterate facial expressions, and inhibit social drinking and eating, eight thousand white insurrectionists trashing the US Capitol and threatening the lives of our leaders, no travel, and the blizzard of bullshit, a.k.a. "fake news."

I frequently woke up in the morning feeling dread, anger, and fear; I felt abused and confused by the system and deeply depressed.

A personal aside: thank you, God, for Grey Goose vodka.

The Inflection Point (In Case You Missed It Earlier)

Somebody—it may have been my friend Steve—emailed me the link to Buddy Hackett's duck joke.

https://www.youtube.com/watch?v=aww4HT5g7ig
YouTube Key Words:
Buddy Hackett duck joke on Carson

I laughed till I hurt. It was an emotional catharsis.

It was also an epiphany. I realized that when I was laughing, I was suddenly not angry, fearful, or depressed. I have watched the duck joke a number of times since. I laugh out loud every time I see it. I had stumbled onto three truisms:

- *Laughter is an instant killer of anger, fear, and depression.*
- *Sans anger and fear, the world is a damn sight more pleasant.*
- *By golly, I can do something about this!*

About the Bawdy Jokes

Since age ten (or younger), I have heard bawdy jokes at grown-up parties, at dinners, at large and small gatherings. I memorized many of them and often jotted down punch lines. What follows are those stories I have remembered that have made me guffaw over the past seventy-five years and enabled me to cause others to laugh out loud. When I'm pissed off, upset, or feeling dread, I often recall one of these punch lines, laugh out loud, and feel my angst instantly evaporate.

I decided to assemble the best bawdy jokes I could recollect and came up with roughly one hundred, of which I believe eighty-three to be thigh-slappers and not totally gross. The other four are a shout-out to limericks, including my two favorites. But eighty-seven jokes do not make a book—hence the eighty-seven patter songs.

The eighty-seven jokes below are starters for this project.

My text is for guidance only. Performers are expected to go off-script and tell the story and punch line in their own words and in a manner that they are most comfortable with. You can do anything or everything that gets the biggest laugh and add your own schticks and signature material.

We all know what jokes are. Not everybody is acquainted with patter songs.

About Patter Songs

Patter songs are recitative songs with tunes. They are

- always chock-a-block full of wicked wit, rhymes, and alliteration;
- often tongue twisters;
- always amusing as hell; and
- always showstoppers.

Patter songs are found on and off Broadway, in opera, vaudeville, and burlesque, on television, in movies, in nightclubs, and of course, in Gilbert and Sullivan operettas.

My Boyhood

In the late 1940s, my grade school put on *All at Sea*, a pastiche of the great Gilbert and Sullivan patter songs. I played Pooh-Bah and had a small speaking part only, but I loved the music—especially the patter songs. My parents saw my delight and took me to New York to see the real deal—two Gilbert and Sullivan operettas (*The Mikado* and *Pinafore*) by the touring company of London's legendary D'Oyly Carte Opera Company. The star was Martyn Green (1899–1975), who always played the lead roles and sang the patter songs with such precise diction that you could understand every word no matter where you were in the theater.

Click below and meet Martyn Green, who was my introduction to patter songs:

IN PERFORMANCE: ALISTAIR COOK AND MARTYN GREEN
https://www.youtube.com/watch?v=mnlcPcVlhvA

- **• IMPORTANT NOTE FOR PRINT-EDITION READERS**
Obviously, you cannot click on the YouTube links provided in this book. Here's what to do when you come to these links for videos:

1. Go to your iPhone, iPad, laptop, desktop computer, or TV.
2. Go to YouTube.
3. Look for the YouTube Key Words I have listed for the video and enter them in the YouTube search bar at the top.
4. In this case, **YouTube Key Words:**

Cook Green patter songs

A Lifetime of Loving Patter Songs

Over the years I have been enthralled by patter songs written and/or performed by verbal wizards. Among them are Danny Kaye (many of whose songs were written by his wife, Sylvia Fine), Noël Coward, Gilbert and Sullivan, Phil Harris, Robert Preston, Madame Spivy, Tom Lehrer, and many wonderful others.

My First Encounter with Danny Kaye

I first became aware of Danny Kaye—and patter songs—in 1942 in the middle of World War II. My parents had gotten involved in producing USO entertainment shows with Broadway performers for the soldiers and sailors stationed in the New York, Long Island, and New Jersey area. One of the shows running at the Imperial Theater at the time was Cole Porter's *Let's Face It* with Danny Kaye, Eve Arden, Nanette Fabray, Vivian Vance, and as a minor understudy, Carol Channing.

It was Kaye's first starring role. Several of the players from the show would come to our house on Long Island late on Saturday nights, spend Sunday and Monday at the beach club, and leave on the noon train for the Monday evening show. I particularly remember Sunnie O'Dea (1918–2002), who played the role of Muriel McGillicuddy.

My parents took me to a *Let's Face It* matinee performance when I was eight—the first play I had ever seen. I loved it! Later in this collection is Danny Kaye's wonderful patter song from the show, "Let's Not Talk About Love."

P.S. *Let's Face It* was made into a truly dreadful movie with a boorish Bob Hope replacing the elegant, charming Danny Kaye. What were they thinking?

Like the experience of hearing bawdy jokes, it's impossible to be angry or fearful when listening to a patter song. So I decided to combine eighty-seven patter songs with the eighty-seven jokes.

Note: I haven't a clue how I ended up with eighty-seven jokes and eighty-seven patter songs. That's how the chips fell.

I believe bawdy jokes, patter songs, and the lowly limerick
are the most fun you can have with the English language.

Whom These Jokes and Patter Songs Are For

- I conceived of this collection for every adult who likes to lighten up a gathering of friends, family, and associates. If you tell jokes, here are eighty-seven—many of which you (hopefully) may not have heard—to add to your repertoire.

- Also, stand-up entertainers, monologists, comics, miscellaneous performers, and happy extroverts can add these jokes to their repertoires and maybe intersperse their routines with patter songs.

- Serious and unserious business executives, lecturers, and teachers can spice up their otherwise ho-hum PowerPoint presentations (in tiny mouse-type) with some new offbeat, off-the-wall material.

Power corrupts. PowerPoint corrupts absolutely."—Edward Tufte

- Improv and traditional theater groups can use this collection as an inspirational workbook and source of unique raw material to create fun evenings and keep their audiences laughing.

An Example of a Delightful Modern Patter Song

One of my favorites is from the Michael Stewart and Cy Coleman musical *Barnum*.

IN PERFORMANCE: MARC GINSBERG
https://www.youtube.com/watch?v=wefP_aEl6_I&t=3s
YouTube Key Words:
Marc Ginsburg museum song

Not Necessary for Many Patter Songs: The Music

With most patter songs, music is non-essential. If you memorize any of these gems and deliver them in a conversational voice with precision—ensuring every word and syllable is heard—you will dazzle your audience.

The Rex Harrison Story

In 1956, when Rex Harrison was offered the part of Professor Henry Higgins in the Broadway musical *My Fair Lady* opposite Julie Andrews playing Liza Doolittle, he initially turned it down. He had never sung in performance. Alan Jay Lerner, Frederick Loewe, and director Moss Hart absolutely wanted Harrison and persuaded him he could do his songs in recitative (singing in the rhythm of ordinary speech with many words on the same note, with music in the background).

For his non-singing role on Broadway (and later in the film opposite Audrey Hepburn), Harrison received Tony, Grammy, Golden Globe, and Academy Awards.

Here's Rex Harrison performing "I'm an Ordinary Man" in recitative:

IN PERFORMANCE: REX HARRISON
https://www.youtube.com/watch?v=wefP_aEl6_I&t=1s
YouTube Key Words:
Ordinary man Rex Harrison

Possible Scenarios for Staging
Bawdy Jokes and Patter Songs

Do it solo—as a teller of stories with boffo punch lines—with or without an accomplice at the piano.

This is no-budget/low-budget entertainment for an intimate theater, a supper club, a living room, or Zoom. In a larger venue, have a cast of three or more people telling stories in their own words, interspersed with patter songs (or patter songs interspersed with jokes).

A Business Model from Old-Time Radio

- One of my favorite radio programs when I was a kid was *Can You Top This?* Four comedians/jokesters told jokes and competed for laughs in front of a live studio audience. Their jokes were rated by the Colgate-Palmolive "Laugh Meter." The show is best remembered—and described on Wikipedia.

THE PLAYERS: Harry Hershfield, Senator (Ed) Ford, Joe Laurie Jr., and host Peter Donald.

https://en.wikipedia.org/wiki/Can_You_Top_This%3F
Google Key Words:
Can You Top This Wikipedia

Audience Participation

It's always a hoot to invite one or more members of the audience onstage, adding to the madness and surprising everybody.

The all-comedy 1812 Productions here in Philly always brings one or more members of the audience onstage to participate in the mayhem.

My favorite example of audience involvement was the solo performance of the great Danish comedian and pianist Victor Borge. At some point in the second half of his Broadway solo show, *Comedy in Music,* Borge would engage—seemingly impromptu—with an audience member and invite him up to the stage.

This supposed audience member was pianist Leonid Hambro, and they would go nuts at the piano together.

https://www.youtube.com/watch?v=VZj-Gp9NKWg
YouTube Key Words:
Hungarian Rhapsody No. 2 Borge and Hambro

How to Intersperse Patter Songs and Jokes

As in Broadway musicals, a joke, a riff, or a punch line can be a cue for a patter song by one or more of the players. Also, a patter song can cue a joke.

IN PERFORMANCE:
Betty Comden and Adolph Green

This idea for zany evenings was partly spurred by seeing the work (live and on YouTube many years later) of the brilliant stage and screen musical comedy duo Betty Comden and Adolph Green (*On the Town, Bells Are Ringing, Singin' in the Rain*, and

The Band Wagon). In 1938 they teamed up with Judy Holliday and a young unknown pianist named Leonard Bernstein to form a troupe called the Revuers. They performed for five years at New York's Village Vanguard and (briefly) the Rainbow Room at the top of the RCA building. As well as creating world-class works for theater and films, Comden and Green put together *A Party*—an intimate two-person evening with a piano accompanist. It played Broadway and in regional theaters all over the country. *A Party* has been captured on YouTube. Watch the performers' antics, interaction, moves, flow, and segues from dialogue to songs for inspiration and guidance. It's a lot of fun.

IN PERFORMANCE: Betty Comden and Adolph Green
https://www.youtube.com/watch?v=8j7sO9DIXOU
YouTube Key Words:
Party Comden Green 1979

Part 2

YOUR STARTER COLLECTION OF
EIGHTY-SEVEN JOKES

1. The Birthday Present

It was Sadie's thirty-fifth birthday, and Moishe left the office at 10:00 a.m. to go out and search for a present. He combed midtown Manhattan and found nothing Sadie would like. Finally, in the lower concourse of the RCA building, he passed a pet shop. In the window was a darling little monkey in a cage.

"Sadie will love this!" Moishe exclaimed to himself. He went into the store and bought the monkey. He paid for the monkey, had the proprietor wrap the cage with birthday paper and a bow, and learned what to feed the monkey.

Moishe gave the pet store owner his address in the Bronx and asked that the monkey be delivered right away.

When Moishe got home to the one-bedroom apartment that afternoon, Sadie was in a dither.

"Did you get my present?"

"Moishe! *A monkey?*"

"Do you like it, Sadie?"

"Moishe, where will it live?"

"It's a new member of the family. He'll live with us!"

"What will it eat?"

"It eats what we eat."

"But where will it sleep?"

"He's a member of the family. He'll sleep with us."

"But Moishe ... *the smell.*"

"Listen, I got used to it. Let the monkey get used to it."

2. Brit Story

An American businessman traveled to London four times a year and always stopped in to see an old college chum from Oxford, now a member of the House of Lords.

When he rang the doorbell, the old family butler answered the door, looking very sad.

"I've come to see Sir Reginald," the American said.

"Oh, he would have loved to see you, but four days ago, Sir Reginald suffered a debilitating stroke and can't talk, can't eat, can barely move, and sleeps most of the day. We are all crushed."

"Can't eat? Then how—"

"Oh, sir, he's being fed through the rectum."

"Oh my God, how awful! I'm here for a week. I'll stop by before I catch the plane to see how he's doing. Maybe he'll be better, and we can have a visit."

The following Sunday, the American rang the doorbell, and the old butler answered, wreathed in smiles, his eyes twinkling with joy.

"How is Sir Reginald?" the businessman asked, handing the old retainer a bouquet of flowers.

"Oh, I'm delighted to tell you his lordship is vastly improved!"

"Is he well enough to have a visitor?"

"Oh, no, sir, I'm afraid not. He still can't talk, he's very weak, and he sleeps most the day. Still being fed through the rectum."

"Well then, how is he better?"

"This morning Sir Reginald fairly snapped at a piece of toast!"

3. A Purely Visual Joke (Acted Out in the Telling)

A guy hit the lottery jackpot and went on a spending spree. He was attractive and young. He exercised daily and had a good physique.

For the first time in his life, he had money to buy a hand-tailored wardrobe and went to the finest tailor in town. He picked out the very best material, and the tailor measured him from toes to neck and showed the guy a photo album of suits he had made for the rich and famous in town. Together they picked out a suit design.

Two weeks later, the suit was ready, and the customer went to pick it up. It looked terrific—really beautiful—with one small problem. The left lapel of the suit jacket stuck out.

The tailor tried to make light of it, but the guy was insistent.

"Okay," said the tailor. "Just tilt your head down on that left lapel, and it will flatten out."

The guy did so, and the lapel was indeed flat under his ear. But then the customer looked in the mirror. "When I tilt my head onto the left lapel, it makes the right sleeve come up my arm, so my whole shirt cuff is exposed."

"You're right," said the tailor. "Tell you what—just scrunch your right arm up to shorten it a bit so the sleeve is just the right length for the shirt cuff."

As the guy was forced to lengthen his left arm, it caused the right pants cuff to rise over his sock.

So the guy was persuaded to bend slightly to shorten his right leg, causing the left pants cuff to go down to the floor, whereupon the guy had to lengthen the left leg.

At the end of the session, the suit fit perfectly, but the guy was a grotesque physical disaster with a long arm and a short arm and a long leg and short leg and a serious limp.

He was not happy. But he left the tailor and started walking down the street like a grossly deformed cripple.

A woman stopped him on the street and exclaimed, "What a beautiful suit!"

"Why, thank you."

"Where did you get it?"

He gave her the tailor's name and address.

"That tailor is a genius," she shrieked. "It's a perfect fit!"

"I don't think he's a genius," the suit owner said.

"Any tailor that can fit a body like that is a genius!"

Two Camel Stories

4. Brick the Camel

In Tripoli an American salesman showed up at the main camel market and told the proprietor he wanted to buy a sturdy, healthy camel for a trip across the Sahara desert.

"I understand there are two kinds of camels: ones that can go six days without water and ones that can last eight days. I need an eight-day camel."

"Sir, all camels can be eight-day camels. You see, when camels get watered just before departure, they generally drink enough to last six days. You have to make sure they drink enough for the extra two days."

"How do I do that?"

"You brick the camel."

"Brick the camel?"

"Sir, when your camel is watering up the morning of your departure, you must stand behind the camel with his testicles between the two bricks. Just when the camel is about to take the last swallow of water, you clap the two bricks hard against his testicles, and he will involuntarily suck up enough additional water to last two extra days."

The American winced and turned pale. "But doesn't that hurt?"

"You have to be careful to keep your thumbs out from between the bricks."

5. The Foreign Legion

A French criminal was given the choice of jail or three years in the Foreign Legion. He chose the Legion and was shipped to a remote post deep in the Sahara desert.

It was tedious, hot, terrible duty, but it beat being in jail. During the first week he asked one of his fellow legionnaires about women.

"We live without them."

He shrugged and went about his duties.

After four weeks he was getting desperate. He said to his comrade, "I'm not sure I can live completely without women. Is there nothing I can do?"

"There's always the camel."

The legionnaire gagged and hung on for another two weeks. Finally, in dire need of relief, he slipped out in the pitch-black desert night and went to the camel shed. The problem was *formidable!*

He stumbled around the shed and found a stepladder, and balancing very carefully on the top step of the ladder, he managed to consummate the act with a very restless, smelly, scratchy animal.

It was disgusting, and he was deeply ashamed of himself.

Two days later, he confided in this colleague what he had done. The fellow legionnaire's eyes bugged out, and he said, *"Mon Dieu! You did what?"*

The man repeated what had happened.

"C'est trés grosse! Yuck!"

"Well, what do you do with the camel?"

"I ride it into town."

6. Flying to Pittsburgh

A middle-aged salesman had to make a last-minute trip to Pittsburgh.

At Newark Airport he got in line at the ticket counter and found himself suddenly obsessing over the fantastically gorgeous blonde dealing with customers—a Marilyn Monroe look-alike with a stunning figure.

When he reached the head of the line, she smiled and said, "May I help you, sir?"

"Yes, I'd like two pickets to Titsburgh."

"Sir?"

"Oh, I'm so sorry. Please forgive me. I'm so embarrassed. I mean two tickets to Pittsburgh."

"Yes, sir," she said cheerfully and printed them out.

The guy paid with his credit card. "I'm so embarrassed," he said to the stranger behind him in line. "I can't believe I said that."

The other man said, "Don't even think about it. Words frequently come out of my mouth when I'm thinking about something else—words I don't mean to say."

"Oh really?"

"For example, just the other morning at breakfast, I meant to ask my wife to pass the salt. But the words that came out of my mouth were 'You fucking bitch, you've ruined my life!'"

7. NFL Fantasy

A couple from Philadelphia traveled to New Orleans for the Super Bowl. As the stadium was filling up, they recognized a fellow Eagles' season ticketholder three seats away. He was an elderly gent and was sitting alone.

"Great to see you!" said the husband. "How come you're alone?"

"My wife passed away," he said sadly.

"Oh, how sorry we are to hear that. But don't you have friends? Someone you could have invited to use your other seat?"

"They're all at the funeral."

8. A Child's Christmas in Grade School

It was the last day of class before the Christmas break. The teacher handed out sheets of drawing paper along with pencils and crayons to her class of young children.

"This is a game," the teacher said after all the materials were distributed. "I want you to draw a picture of your favorite Christmas carol," she said. "Think of a Christmas carol. Think of the words and draw a picture of what you think. It can be whatever you like—'Little Town of Bethlehem,' 'Hark the Herald Angels Sing,' 'The First Noel,' 'Away in the Manger,' 'We Three Kings.' After twenty-five minutes I will say, 'Stop!' and you will hand in your drawings. Then I will hold up each picture, and the class will have to guess the Christmas carol. Ready, set ... start now! You have twenty-five minutes!"

The kids began furiously drawing and coloring. Twenty-five minutes later, the teacher said, "Stop! Let's see what wonderful things you've done!"

As each drawing was held up for everybody to see, the child who drew it raised a hand to be identified, and the class guessed what the Christmas carol was.

Up came a picture of the crèche—Baby Jesus, Mary, a shepherd, and three kings. In the very center of the picture, dominating the scene, was a very large, very fat man. Nobody in the class could guess the song.

"We are stumped! What is the Christmas carol?" the teacher asked the moppet.

"Silent Night."

"And who is this?" asked the teacher, pointing to the big fellow in the center.

"That's Round John Virgin."

9. You're in the Army Now

A bunch of raw recruits got off the bus at the army base and were ordered to line up. A tough old senior sergeant started pacing up and down in front of them.

"What did you do for a living before you enlisted in the army?"

"I was a cork soaker."

"A what?"

"Cork soaker."

"What the hell is a cork soaker?"

"I worked for a winery, and before corks are inserted into a bottle, they are dry and hard. My job was to soak them in water until they became softer and pliable so they could be pushed into the opening."

"And you," he said to another recruit, "what did you do?"

"I was a coke sacker."

"A what?"

"Coke sacker. I worked for a drug cartel. After opium was processed into cocaine, it was stored in bulk. My job was to put the coke into sacks."

"And you?"

"I'm a sock tucker."

"A what?"

"Sock tucker. I worked in a mill where socks were manufactured. Socks are made one at a time, and my job was pairing them up and tucking the tops into one another, so the pairs could be packaged together."

A young recruit farther down the line raised his hand. "Call on me, Sarge. I'm the real thing."

Five Doctor Jokes

10. Hondas

An older guy was farting Hondas.

That's right, Hondas. Every time he broke wind (and it was often), the sound came out a roaring *H-O-N-D-A-A-A!*

He went to his regular family doctor, who gave him a clean bill of health.

"But what about my Honda farting problem?"

The doctor looked in the guy's mouth and gave him the name of a Chinese dentist.

"What? A Chinese dentist?"

"Just do it. He'll take care of you."

An hour later, the guy was in the chair of the Chinese dentist, who looked in his mouth.

"Ah, abscess!" he exclaimed. "Need to fix."

"What's an abscess on a tooth have to do with my digestive tract?"

"Abscess make the fart go Honda!"

11. Mother's Milk

Hymie, forty-eight years old from Brooklyn, came down with a mysterious illness. Feeling terrible all the time, he went to different doctors and hospitals for test after test. Nothing turned up.

Finally, the doctors at Beth Israel discovered the problem: a rare degenerative disease for which a cure had only recently been found.

"Vat's the cure?" Hymie asked the doctor.

"Mother's milk."

"Vat?"

"Mother's milk. I've got to prescribe for you a vet nurse."

"A vet nurse?"

"You go home, Hymie, and she'll come to your house this afternoon."

That afternoon the doorbell rang, and a large woman was standing at the door and introduced herself as the "vet nurse."

She was very tall, and Hymie was very short. She came into the living room and sat on the sofa and motioned for Hymie to come sit on her lap. Then she unbuttoned her blouse and revealed an enormous pair of breasts busting with milk.

"Vat should I do?" Hymie asked.

"Suck," she said.

Hymie started sucking, harder and harder. The wet nurse began to get excited. "Is there something more I can do for you?"

Hymie, slurping happily, shook his head in the negative.

"Nothing? You're sure there's nothing more I can do for you?"

He shook his head in the negative again and continued to suck.

"*Please!* Isn't there something—anything—I can do for you?"

Slurp … slurp. Hymie looked up. "You have maybe a cookie?"

12. "What are the three advantages of mother's milk as opposed to a store-bought formula?" a distinguished bespectacled pediatrician asked a class of expectant mothers. He was a very serious, stern academic gentleman.

There was silence from the audience.

"Mother's milk is produced by nature especially for your child.

"Mother's milk is portable; it goes everywhere and is immediately available.

"And it comes in such cute containers."

13. Danger in the Woods

Two hunters were out looking for deer, and after a long morning, Charlie leaned his deer rifle against a tree and started to take a much-needed leak.

An unseen snake in the grass suddenly uncoiled, rose up, and bit Charlie on the end of his penis. Screaming in pain, he yelled, "Joe, Joe, I've been bit by a snake! Get me to a doctor."

"Charlie, there's no doctors around here. We're deep in the woods!"

"Call 9-1-1 for God's sake. Tell them to put a doctor on the phone and ask him what to do! The pain is killing me. I'm gonna die!"

Joe dialed 9-1-1, and the emergency operator forwarded the call to a local hospital, where an ER physician came on the line. Joe explained what had happened. "He's in great pain and thinks he's gonna die!"

"What kind of snake?" the ER doctor said.

"I got no idea."

"What'd it look like? I gotta know if it's venomous or not. Did your friend see it?"

"I'm in pain!" Charlie cried. "I'm gonna die."

"Charlie, what did the snake look like?"

"I'm gonna die!"

"The snake—what'd it look like?"

Between gasps of pain, Charlie described the snake hysterically, and Joe repeated the description over the cell phone.

"My God, that's a highly venomous snake," the doctor said. "You've gotta get the venom out right away, or your friend will die."

"How do I get the venom out?"

"You've gotta suck it out."

"Suck it out how?"

"Do you have a knife?"

"Yeah."

"Sharp?"

"Yeah, sharp. I use it for skinning deer."

"Here's what you do," the doctor on the phone said. "Take the knife, and where the snake bit the guy, cut an X in the skin where the snake bit."

"Then what?"

"Then suck the venom out. Suck real hard, harder than you've sucked anything in your life. Do it right now, or your friend's gonna die."

Joe put the phone down.

"What'd the doctor say, Joe? What'd he say?"

"You're gonna die, Charlie."

14. Premarital Physical Checkup

A middle-aged spinster who had never been with a man found a gentleman who wanted to marry her. She went to her gynecologist for a checkup.

The woman had an enormous mouth, and every question and every answer was articulated through this oversized oral orifice.

Toward the end of the exam, she said, "NOW, DOCTOR, YOU KNOW I HAVE NEVER … NEVER BEEN WITH A MAN. AND I HAVE NO IDEA ABOUT MY FIANCÉ'S PENIS. IS THERE ANY WAY OF KNOWING HOW, UH … HOW BIG IT IS WITHOUT ACTUALLY SEEING IT?"

"Why, yes," the doctor said quietly. "In developmental stages, the male nose and the male penis are in the same growth canal. A man with a large nose very often has a large penis."

"OH REALLY, DOCTOR? THAT'S FASCINATING!" She paused and said, "IF THAT'S TRUE ABOUT MEN, IS THERE ANY WAY A MAN CAN KNOW THE SIZE OF A … A WOMAN'S VAGINA?"

"Well, as a matter of fact, yes. The mouth and the vagina are at opposite ends of the same bodily canal. So a woman with a very large mouth can be expected to have a very large vagina."

The woman made a tiny circle with her mouth and said very quietly, "Oh really, Doctor?"

15. Jewish Funeral

Avraham died.

He had been a terrible human being—mean, penny-pinching, hated children and dogs, a nasty drunk, got into fights. Never married. No children.

Avraham did not have a regular temple. He was not religious. A small scattering of people showed up at the funeral home for the service.

A rabbi who had never met the deceased delivered an all-purpose homily and led the pathetically small group in prayers.

Finally, the rabbi turned to the few folks and asked if someone in the congregation would say a few words about Avraham.

Nobody raised a hand.

Again, the rabbi asked for someone to say something.

Nothing.

In desperation he asked one more time. "Please, won't somebody—*anybody*—say something about Avraham!"

A little old man in the back row tentatively raised his hand.

"Yes!" the rabbi shouted. "You, sir! What can you say about Avraham?"

The man stood up and said, "His brudder vas voise." [His brother was worse.]

16. A Gross of Gross Dinner Napkins

A sweet little gray-haired lady walked into the legendary F. Schumacher fabric store in New York City. The clerk asked, "May I help you?"

"Yes," she said sweetly, "I want twelve dozen double-damask dinner napkins."

"Certainly, madam. Come look at these samples and choose the ones you want."

The lady found what she wanted, and the sales lady said, "Do you want them embroidered?"

"Yes, I do," she said. "I want in capital letters F-U-C-K-M-E."

"Excuse me, madam?"

"I said F-U-C-K-M-E."

"Why, we can't do that! That's disgusting. You will ruin our reputation!"

The little woman looked quizzical and pained.

"I don't understand. These are for the *First Unitarian Church of Kennebunkport, Maine.*"

17. Holiday Plans

A British aristocrat was getting a haircut from his regular insouciant Cockney barber.

"Me an' m' missus is goin' to Brighton for our 'oliday."

"That's nice."

"You goin' way for 'oliday?"

"Yes, as a matter of fact, we are going to Italy."

"It'ly? Well, la-di-dah. Why would you want to go to It'ly when you could go to Brighton?"

"We like the weather, and we especially like the wine."

"Oh, you like the wine," the barber said, his voice dripping with sarcasm. "So la-di-dah, you're too good for Brighton."

He finished the haircut. One month later, the guy returned for another haircut.

"And so did you go to It'ly like you said you was going?"

"Yes, I did. It was lovely."

"An' I suppose you went to see the pope."

"In fact, I did."

"An' did you talk to the pope?"

"As a matter of fact, yes, I did."

"Oh, you did! And wot did the pope say to you?"

"What did the pope say to me?"

"Yes, wot did the pope say to you?" The sneer in his voice was palpable.

"The pope said, 'That's a fucking awful haircut you got.'"

18. A Ballerina's Final Performance

The greatest Russian ballerina of the century was a woman named Ludmilla. She was famous for her leaps, pirouettes, and splits and beloved for her exquisite technique.

Alas, she was retiring, and her farewell performance was dazzling.

She did reprises from all her great performances to shrieks of joy and wild applause. Finally, at the end of the evening, she ascended to the first balcony on a rope ladder, did several elegant moves, and then leapt from the balcony to the stage below, where she landed in a full split.

The theater went wild. The curtain went up and down numerous times, but something was wrong. Wreathed in smiles but grimacing in pain, Ludmilla remained in the split position on the stage apron, bowing and nodding while the crowd screamed and stomped.

When the curtain came down for the last time and all the backstage people came to congratulate her, she remained in her spilt.

Finally, Boris, her devoted manager for thirty years, leaned down and whispered in her ear, "Ludmilla, darling, it's over. You can get up now."

"Oh, Boris, Boris," she muttered softly in her thick Russian accent. "Boris, rock me gently to break the suction!"

19. A Royal Arrival

Her Majesty the Queen drove to Victoria Station in her coach and four, accompanied by postilions and surrounded by a contingent of royal horse guards.

She was going to greet the prime minister of Australia and bring him back to the palace for lunch.

As Her Majesty and the Aussie prime minister headed down the mall toward Buckingham Palace, making polite small talk and giving little hand-circle waves to pedestrians along the way, all four horses, seemingly in unison, let fly a series of farts with a deafening roar that sounded like a jet fighter breaking the sound barrier. This was followed by a truly horrific odor wafting over the entire entourage.

"How very embarrassing," Her Majesty said quietly. "I'm so very sorry."

"Think nothing of it, Your Majesty," said the Aussie prime minister. "Actually, ma'am, I thought it was the horses."

20. Conversation Starter

At a western dude ranch, a very shy young man was smitten with a gorgeous young woman guest.

They went horseback riding in a small group one morning. The pair chatted amiably about the scenery and their careers as they rode along. The dude was shy and could not bring himself to say anything personal.

He went to the wrangler for a suggestion on how to break the ice.

"You must engage her in conversation," the wrangler said. "I'll tell you what. Tomorrow morning, I will paint your horse's genitals bright red. When you go out together, she will notice the red patch on the hind end of the horse and comment on it. That can lead to a discussion of the horse's genitals, and that can lead to a discussion of genitals in general, which leads to sex, and you're on your way to beginning a meaningful conversation."

The next morning, the deed was done, and the horse's genitals were bright red.

Alas, the horses were facing each other when the man and the guest mounted, and the pair rode off. She never noticed the red paint. The conversation never took place.

The desperate young dude, now obsessing over the girl, told the wrangler what had happened. He was beside himself, especially since he had heard the girl of his dreams was leaving in two days.

"Okay, I'll paint the entire underbelly of the horse red as well as the genitals. That will result in her noticing the red belly, which will lead to a discussion of red genitals, which will bring up the mating of horses, and you can take it from there."

The next morning, the sun was very bright. She mounted her horse while squinting and looking away from the sun. She never saw the horse's red belly.

Back in the wrangler's office, the now-crazed dude said, "Ya gotta do something! She's leaving tomorrow."

The wrangler said, "Okay, I'll paint the entire horse red."

The next morning, the girl walked to the paddock, blinked, and exclaimed, "Goodness, look at the red horse!"

"Yeah, let's fuck."

21. A Lesson in Tact

George was a young sailor in the US Navy stationed on a destroyer in the Pacific. His job was to be the voice of the ship's public address system.

One morning a message came into the radio shack that Seaman Malloy's mother back in the States had died suddenly.

George immediately got on the public address and announced to the entire ship's company, "Attention! Attention! Seaman Malloy, your mother has just died! To repeat! Seaman Malloy, your mother has just died. Your mother is dead!"

Malloy, who was in his bunk, sat bolt upright, smacked his head on the metal bunk bottom overhead, suffered a concussion, and was evacuated to an aircraft carrier with a large sick bay.

George was brought up before the captain and severely rebuked for his gross insensitivity. He was not court-martialed, but he was required to go through a training program on human relations and, above all, tact. He should *never* deliver a deeply intimate and personal message over the public address system.

Six weeks later, a message came over the radio that Seaman Perez's mother had died.

George immediately hit the switch and started to announce that Seaman Perez's mother had died. Suddenly remembering the trouble he'd gotten into two months prior, George said, "Attention, attention! All hands on deck! All hands on deck. Assemble on the fantail to hear an important announcement!"

The ship's company lined up in precise ranks at the stern of the ship.

George, carrying a large bullhorn, appeared on the upper deck overlooking the mass of officers and crew who had gathered and were standing at attention.

"Attention! Attention!" he shouted into the bullhorn.

Suddenly, there was silence.

"All men who have mothers, take one step forward!"

Pause.

"Not so fast, Perez!"

Zoo Stories

22. Central Park Zoo

A grandmother and her young grandson were standing in front of the porcupine cage, where two species of porcupine were sunning themselves.

The grandmother turned to a zookeeper nearby and asked, "How do you tell the two species of porcupine from each other?"

"Oh, well, actually, madam …" He leaned his mop against the wall and held up both hands with forefingers extended. "It all depends on their pricks. The porcupine on the right has a prick about this long," he said, holding his two index fingers three inches apart. "And the porcupine on the left has a prick this long," he said, holding is fingers eight inches apart.

"How dare you talk like in front of me and my grandson! I'm going to complain to the director of the zoo!"

Grandma and grandson marched off to the office of the zoo's president, barged inside, and strode over to the window.

"Do you see that man down there—that despicable, foul-talking man?" She then told the story of how he had talked about the size of porcupines' pricks.

"Madam, please calm down. This is not an educated man. He feeds animals and cleans cages. He made a mistake."

"He certainly did!"

"He should have used the word *quill*. What he meant to say is the porcupine on the right has *quills* this long, and the one on the left has quills this long. Actually, they both have pricks about two inches long."

23. San Diego Zoo

At the San Diego Zoo the male gorilla was aged and weak—no longer able to perform duties as a stud. A nubile female gorilla was coming into her estrous cycle, and the zoo's management was desperate to repopulate the primate collection.

"What can we do?" the director asked helplessly.

His assistant looked out the window and saw one of the zookeepers cleaning a cage. He was a big, hulking ape of a man with long, long arms, a blank stare, and a projecting lower jaw. "How about him?" the assistant said. "He doesn't make much money. I'll bet we could pay him to be the father."

The director went to the window and immediately agreed. "How much money should we offer him?"

"I'll bet he would do it for $200."

"Ask him," the director said.

The assistant director took the ape-like zookeeper over to the primate section, pointed out the young female, and propositioned the man.

"For $200?"

"That's right, $200."

With a quizzical, confused expression, the zookeeper stood in silence, staring long and hard at the female gorilla. At length he said, "You want me to do it for $200?"

"Yes, $200."

The zookeeper stared at the female ape for a good three minutes. "Okay. But I can't do it for three weeks."

"You have to do it in the next four days. She's in estrous. Why do you want three weeks?"

"I need time to come up with the $200."

24. Bronx Zoo

A mother, father, and young son went to the zoo. At the elephant enclosure the father excused himself and went to the men's room.

Mother and son stood looking at a huge male African elephant.

"Mom, what's the thing hanging down?" the kid asked.

"Why, that's his trunk."

"No, no, the other thing hanging down."

"Oh, that's his tail."

"No, I don't mean the tail. That big thing in the middle hanging down."

The mother was embarrassed and said, "Oh, it's … it's nothing."

The family went around the zoo and were going by the elephant enclosure again when the mother excused herself and went to the ladies' room.

Standing in the center of the enclosure was that same giant African elephant.

"Daddy, what's that big thing hanging down?"

"That's the elephant's trunk."

"No, I mean at the other end."

"Why, that's the elephant's tail."

"No, not the tail. That thing in the middle. Mommy said it was nothing."

"Your mother is spoiled."

25. Do Brits Have a Sense of Humor?

An American tourist in London told a joke to three friends, once of whom was a Brit.

"It seems a young girl was standing on the sidewalk when three men went by her on the street—a man on a horse, a man walking, and a man on a bicycle. Which one knew the girl?"

"I have no idea."

"The horse manure!"

Later that day the Brit told this American story to two Brit friends.

"This young girl was standing by the side of the road when three men went by—a pedestrian, an equestrian, and a cyclist. Which one knew her?"

Both Brits shrugged and said they had no idea.

"For some strange reason the answer was horseshit."

26. My Wife Is Losing Her Hearing

At the finish of a routine medical exam, Harry said, "By the way, Doctor, I think my wife is becoming deaf, and I'm not sure what to do."

"Why do you think she's getting deaf?"

"When I speak to her, she doesn't reply. I don't want to hurt her in any way, but I need some guidance."

"I need to know more," the doctor said. "When you go in the front door tonight, ask her in a loud voice what's for dinner."

"Then what?"

"If she doesn't answer, get closer and ask her again. Keep asking as you get closer and closer. Let me know how close you have to be to her before she answers."

Harry went home. Inside the front door he shouted, "Honey, what's for dinner?"
No reply.

He went into the dining room and shouted, "Sweetie, what's for dinner?"
No reply.

Finally, in the kitchen where he was face-to-face with her, he asked again. "Honey, what's for dinner?"

"For the third time, chicken."

27. Posnanski the Bridge Builder

Joe Posnanski was on the 102nd-floor observation deck of the Empire State building, showing the sights to a cousin visiting from Poland.

"See that tunnel entrance down there? That's the Queens Midtown Tunnel. I was a sand hog on that tunnel.

"Now look over there. That skyscraper is the Citibank building. I spent two years on the construction crew of that building.

"That bridge over there—Queensboro Bridge. I helped build that bridge."

Posnanski's cousin said he was impressed.

"Don't be impressed," Posnanski told his cousin. "Let me tell you about America. Do they call me Posnanski the digger of tunnels? No. Do they call me Posnanski the builder of skyscrapers? No. Do the call me Posnanski the bridge builder? No. But suck one little cock …"

Gallows Humor

28. The king of a very small kingdom inherited a court jester from his late father. The jester's stock-in-trade was being a punster. His endless puns drove the king and court crazy. Finally, the king called him in and said, "If you make one more public pun, I will execute you—death by hanging." The jester's silence lasted seventy-two hours, and then he came up with a pun, whereupon the king ordered him to be hanged.

The day came, and a huge crowd gathered to view the execution. The rope was around the jester's neck when the king had a change of heart. The jester had been employed by the crown for six decades and had been a favorite of the king's father. At the last minute the king ordered a halt to the execution. The hangman loosened the knot and removed the rope from around the clown's neck. The condemned man stepped forward and shouted to the king, "Thank you, Your Majesty!"

Unable to help himself, the Jester shouted to the crowd, "No noose is good noose!"

And then they hanged him.

29. Be Careful What You Wish For

A salesman in Boston had just lost a million-dollar order to an arch competitor and was really depressed. He walked into Cheers on Beacon Street, sat down at the bar, and ordered a triple bourbon neat.

The bartender placed the hefty drink in front of the salesman and said, "Jeez, pal, you look real unhappy."

The salesman told him about the lost million-dollar order.

"You need cheering up!" said the bartender. Reaching under the bar, he pulled out a beautiful miniature Steinway grand piano. He placed the one-foot-tall piano and a six-inch-high bench on the bar in front of the salesman.

The sad-sack salesman sat back and asked, "What's this?"

"You watch," said the bartender. Then he brought out a tiny one-foot-tall piano player dressed in a brown checked suit and a brown bowler hat. The tiny foot-high musician sat down on the wee bench and began pounding out ragtime tunes and boogie-woogie on the little Steinway.

The salesman burst out laughing and yelled, "Where'd you get this?"

"I made a wish."

"Huh?"

"Yesterday I was walking my dog on Revere Beach and came across a beautiful antique bottle. I picked it up and brought it here. I mentioned it to a patron, and he asked if he could see the bottle. I said sure and pulled it out from under the bar. I must have rubbed it or something, because when I set it on the bar, a genie came out of the bottle and told me to make a wish."

"And what happened?"

"The genie said I had ten seconds to make one wish. 'It's your only wish,' he said. 'If you don't make a wish in ten seconds, your opportunity is gone.' I blurted out my wish and *bang*! This tiny piano and ragtime player appeared on the bar, and I've had them since yesterday."

"Do you still have the bottle?"

"Yeah." He pulled the bottle out and set it on the bar.

"If I rub the bottle, will the genie appear?"

"I don't know. Try it."

The salesman rubbed the bottle, and the genie popped out.

"You have ten seconds from now to make a wish. If you don't make a wish in ten seconds, you'll never get another chance."

"I … I … uh … wish for a … a … oh, jeez … I wish for … for a million bucks."

Bang! Suddenly, ducks appeared everywhere, filling the bar. They sat on all the bar stools, tables, and chairs and snaked out the door and across Beacon Street, covering much of the Boston Public Garden on the other side of the street.

The quacking was deafening, and suddenly duck doo-doo was everywhere. The smell was disgusting and overpowering.

Over the racket of quacking, crapping ducks, the salesman yelled at the top of his voice, "Hey, I asked for a million *bucks*, not a million ducks!"

The bartender shouted back, "You don't think for a minute that I asked for a twelve-inch pianist!"

Two Golf Jokes

30. An Unlikely Pair

Golf was Bill Brown's life. He traveled the world and managed to play seventy-two of the one hundred greatest courses in the world, from Scotland's R&A to Pebble Beach to Wack-Wack in the Philippines. In his late middle age, after a lifetime of marvelous health and eyesight like an eagle, Bill began having trouble following the ball. A visit to the eye doctor confirmed the problem: macular degeneration.

Bill continued to play until he could no longer see the ball beyond a few feet. With great sorrow he went into his club's golf shop and confessed to the pro—a dear friend and teacher of forty-three years—that he could no long see the ball and was being forced to give up the game, whereupon he began to sob.

The pro said, "Wait a minute, Bill. You heard Jack has come down with Alzheimer's.

If you become a twosome, you can go out together. You can hit the ball with your magnificent swing, and Jack, who can see perfectly, can guide you to the ball, and you can continue playing."

That afternoon, Bill and Jack paired off. On the first tee, Jack let fly a magnificent shot 220 yards down the middle of the fairway.

When it was Bill's turn, he hooked it slightly, and the ball went into the second cut of rough 240 yards away.

As they started down the fairway, Bill said, "Jack, did you see it?"

"Absolutely."

They walked toward the green and found Jack's ball smack in the middle of the fairway. Jack's iron shot put the ball fifteen feet from the hole.

"Did you see my ball, Jack?"

"Absolutely."

"Where'd it go?"

"I forget."

31. Devotion to Golf

It was July 4. Only a total fanatic would go golfing on the busiest day of the year when the course would be mobbed. Paul and George decided to beat the crowds and go out real early. Sunrise was 5:27 a.m., and they were scheduled to tee off at 6:00 a.m.

Paul and George began their trek around the completely quiet course on a beautiful morning. On the third fairway, George dropped dead of a heart attack. Paul tried to revive him, but it was obvious George was gone.

Six hours later, Paul was in the club dining room and looked terrible—pale and absolutely wiped out. He was nursing a cold beer.

A good friend caught sight of him and went over to the table. "Paul, you look terrible. Are you okay?"

"Worst day of my life," Paul said.

"What happened?"

"George died on the third fairway."

"Oh, I'm so sorry. George was your oldest friend."

"Terrible day! Hit the ball, drag George. Hit the ball, drag George."

32. One Joke, Two Punch Lines, Punch Line #1

The Royal Explorers' Club of London was having a gala dinner honoring the oldest and most distinguished member, Sir Percy Adams, now age ninety-two, frail but spry and very alert. It was white-tie, with all medals and decorations worn. The meal would be followed by a conversation with the honoree, a legendary explorer and survivor of forty-seven big-game hunting trips to Africa.

Following the lively dinner, Sir Percy and the club president came onstage and sat down in easy chairs, each with a microphone.

"Sir Percy, what was your most terrifying experience?"

"In Kenya. With my two gun-bearers on either side of me, I came to a large clearing in the woods. Suddenly, out of nowhere, a huge angry lioness charged us. The gun bearer to my right dropped his rifle and fled. Same thing with the gun bearer to my left. I was alone in the clearing with only my pistol. The lioness—you could see the fury in her eyes and her roar was deafening! She leapt at me and … and … *ee-yow!* Oh my God! I shit in my pants!"

"I'm not surprised, Sir Percy. If I were in your shoes, I probably would have soiled—"

"No, no, you fool! Not then, just now!"

33. One Joke, Two Punch Lines, Punch Line #2

"So what happened, Sir Percy?"

"As she charged me, I fired off six shots from my pistol—and missed! But the lioness some how didn't touch me. Can you believe it? As she came at me, I ducked. This fierce huntress jumped over me and missed me completely and ran into the woods!

"I immediately went back to my tent, ordered a box of fifty rounds of ammunition for the pistol, and fired fifty rounds for practice. That won't happen again!"

"Did you ever see the lioness again?"

"As a matter of fact, yes. I came out of the woods and came to another clearing and saw the lioness."

"And what was she doing?"

"Practicing jumps."

Two Geezer Stories

34. Growing Old

Two old geezers were discussing their health and daily routines.

"I wake up every morning at nine, and it's a struggle. A swollen prostate makes it difficult and painful to urinate. And I suffer terribly from constipation. It's really a horrible life."

"Those are not my problems," the other geezer said. "I wake up every morning at seven, and my pee is as strong as the leaping, roaring, rushing, gushing of waters of

Niagara Falls pouring into the Niagara River. And oh, my bowels perform absolutely wonderfully, loose and easy!"

"Every morning at seven?"

"Every morning at seven, yes. Like clockwork."

"God, how I envy you."

"Don't."

"Why do you say that?"

"I don't get up until nine."

35. The Costs of Old Age

An older gentleman in a limousine arrived at the Mustang Ranch outside of Reno, Nevada, and asked the hourly price of a companionable lady.

"How old are you, sir?" asked the receptionist.

"Eighty-four."

"Twenty dollars for every year of your life."

"Why, that's … $1,680 an hour!"

"Yes, sir."

"You're putting me on!"

"That's extra."

36. Churchillian Lore

One day in the middle of World War II, a member of the War Cabinet, Clement Attlee—whose official title was Lord Privy Seal—was desperate to see Prime Minister Winston Churchill immediately. Churchill had disappeared somewhere deep in the Houses of Parliament. "Find Winston," Atlee said to one of his aides. The young man went searching all over and eventually detected a faint whiff of cigar smoke. He followed the aromatic trail and realized it was coming out from under the door of a small, out-of-the-way loo Churchill was known to frequent when he had to get away to think. He banged on the door and Churchill growled, "Who is it?"

"Prime Minister, the Lord Privy Seal needs to see you at once, Sir."

"Tell the Lord Privy Seal I am sealed to the privy," Churchill snarled, "and I can only deal with one shit at a time."

Celebrity Stories

George S. Kaufman

One of the great wits of the 1920s, '30s, and '40s was playwright George S. Kaufman. Kaufman and his longtime collaborator Moss Hart wrote such classics as *The Man Who Came to Dinner* and *George Washington Slept Here.*

37. When Kaufman showed up at Moss Hart's ranch in Arizona, Hart was duded up in a traditional cowboy outfit—chaps, decorated western shirt, giant Stetson hat, and gorgeous tooled leather cowboy boots with solid silver spurs.

Kaufman's comment: "Hi-Yo Platinum!"

38. In 1943 George S. Kaufman and a friend were in Times Square when they saw a huge billboard announcing the opening of *The Outlaw*—a film directed by Howard Hughes, legendary pilot and owner of RKO Studios. The centerpiece of this massive billboard was a giant photograph of the star Hughes had signed—Jane Russell.

Hughes was famous in Hollywood and New York for his fascination with women's breasts. Hughes had actually designed a special brassiere for Jane Russell that would show off her considerable mammary endowments without risking the wrath of the censors.

Kauffman and his companion stood staring at the gargantuan reclining figure of Jane Russell on the billboard.

"Hughes mis-titled the film," Kaufman said. "*The Outlaw* is wrong."

"What should the movie be called?" the other guy asked.

"*The Sale of Two Titties.*"

39. Kaufman was also a champion bridge player and a regular at the two great New York citadels of bridge, the Regency and Cavendish Clubs.

Once a bridge partner made a hash of playing a hand, and Kaufman got angrier and angrier.

At the end, the partner said, "Okay, George, how would you have played that hand?"

"Under an assumed name."

40. When another bridge partner was dummy, he announced to Kaufman that he was going to the men's room.

"It's the first time tonight I'll know what you have in your hand."

41. Edward VII

The oldest son of Queen Victoria was Prince Edward, who eventually became King Edward VII when Victoria passed. Edward was a notorious womanizer who had a string of mistresses, the most famous affair being a long-term relationship with Lilly Langtry. She was a stunning British American socialite, producer, and actress. The story is told that one morning they were together at breakfast, and Edward was going over his expenses. He looked up and exclaimed, "Good heavens, Lilly, I've spent enough on you to buy a battleship!"

"Yes, and you've spent enough in me to float one!"

42. Margaret Thatcher

The longest-serving prime minister of England was Margaret Thatcher—articulate, brilliant, and savage. It has been said that when she was finished handling the pugnacious members of the House of Commons during question time, one had to take care not to slip and take a spill on the testicles that were rolling around on the House floor.

Once when she was at a dinner with her chief ministers at Rule's Restaurant on Maiden Lane, the maître d' asked for Mrs. Thatcher's order.

"I'll have the prime rib," she said.

"And what about the vegetables?"

"They'll have the prime rib also."

43. LBJ

When Senate Majority Leader Lyndon Johnson ascended to the presidency after the assassination of John F. Kennedy, he did not want to give up his membership in the Democratic Senate Caucus. The members were all friends of his—often of many years—and he wanted to remain close to them.

As president, he was now chief executive of the second branch of government and had to give up all ties to the House.

But he campaigned hard, giving the legendary "Johnson Treatment" to each of his pals in the Democratic caucus, urging them to make an exception and vote to reinstate him.

Shortly before the caucus went into session to vote, a reporter asked Johnson how the vote would go.

"Everybody loves the idea," Johnson said. "They'll vote me in seventeen to nothing."

The vote was sixteen to one against Johnson. The single yes vote was Johnson's.

"Mr. President, what happened?" asked the reporter who had heard his prediction of unanimity. "You said the vote would be seventeen to zero in favor, and it was sixteen to one against."

"Son, today I learned the difference between a cactus and a caucus."

"The difference between a cactus and a caucus, Mr. President?"

"With a cactus, all the pricks are on the outside."

44. Will Rogers

When Will Rogers, the great folksy American trick rope artist, comedian, and star of *Ziegfeld Follies*, was a small boy, he was sitting on a fence at the family ranch in Oklahoma on the shore of Lake Oologah.

Suddenly, a magnificent prize stud bull from the next ranch was being led across the Rogers property by two cowhands.

"Where are you going?" young Will asked.

"We're taking this bull over to the next ranch to service a prize heifer," one of them replied.

Will Rogers often said, "Now every time I hear the word 'service,' I know somebody is going to get screwed."

45. The Rich and Powerful

One of the richest bankers in New York had a Chinese cook whose popovers were legendary—the talk of New York high society. With a light crust, fluffy, and hot inside, they were delicious. The recipe was secret. Neither the banker nor his chef would reveal the recipe.

At a large black-tie dinner party made up of bankers, brokers, and financiers, one of the moguls excused himself, ostensibly to go to the loo. Instead, he slipped into the mammoth kitchen, sidled up to the Chinese chef, and proffered a fat wad of hundred-dollar bills. "Ping, the popover recipe."

The cook's eyes bugged out, and he said, "Yes, sir."

The titan pulled out a small pad of paper and a gold Cross pen.

"First you put flour in a mixing bowl," the chef said.

"How much flour?"

"Two and one-quarter cups."

The guy started scribbling. "Then what?"

"Add water."

"How much water?"

"It must be cold water, very cold."

"Exactly how much cold water, Ping?"

"About two mouthfuls."

46. True Story: A Public Relations Oops

On March 4, 1889, a pig-iron salesman named Phineas P. Jenkins spent the night on a railroad sleeper car and woke up the next morning covered with bedbug bites. He sent a very angry, deeply insulting letter of complaint to the Pullman Company. He threatened a lawsuit and said he was going to write letters to every major newspaper in America describing his horrible night on the Pullman. By return mail he received a very long and deeply moving, heartfelt letter of apology from the executive offices of Pullman Company in Chicago. It described how bedbugs were the number one problem the company faced and went into great detail about all the systems in place (including weekly sanitizing of all bedding). This happened very, very seldom, and it was mortifying. Amazingly, the letter was personally signed by George M. Pullman, president of the Pullman Palace Car Company. Phineas Jenkins was dazzled at receiving a deeply personal mea culpa letter from the president of the company. He immediately felt better—until a little piece of yellow paper fluttered out of the envelope and landed in his lap. It was a handwritten note: *Susy, send this son of a bitch the bedbug letter. GMP*

Five Restaurant Stories

47. It Helps to Speak French

A guy went into a restaurant for a light lunch, and the waitress handed him a menu. When she came back, the patron said, "I'd like a quickie."

The waitress was shocked. "What did you say?"

"I'd like to have a quickie."

The waitress hauled off and socked the patron in the face and stormed into the kitchen.

All conversation stopped, and the room went silent.

A guy at the adjoining table said, "Sir, I think you meant to order a quiche. That's pronounced 'keesh.'"

48. Upmarket Restaurant

After a harrowing twelve-hour day in Omaha 1,500 miles from his home, a tired and cranky salesman stumbled into a nondescript restaurant, desperate for a couple of drinks and dinner before going back to his hotel.

He went through the revolving door, and the interior was elegant—with white tablecloths, shiny silver utensils, and sparkling glassware on every table, damask wall coverings, and beautiful artwork everywhere.

"Welcome, sir," said the maître d' in a warm, soothing tone. "Allow me to take your coat. Sit anywhere you like."

The guy sat down at a table across from the bar. A waiter in a tuxedo came over and placed a wedge of excellent French brie and a plate of crackers on the table. The waiter was so upbeat and oh-so-nice.

"Welcome, sir," he gushed. "How delighted we are to see you. May I bring you a drink or a glass of wine perhaps?"

"A Bombay Sapphire martini up with olive, extra dry, served very cold, shaken, not stirred."

"Yes, sir! Right away, sir!"

The salesman was delighted by the warmth and enthusiasm of everyone on the restaurant staff.

The sound of the cocktail shaker was music to the salesman's ears. The martini arrived and was glorious. The glass was frosted, and a hint of dry vermouth took the sharp edge off the gin.

After about five minutes, the waiter quietly sidled up to the table and presented a big, elegantly designed menu. "Take your time—there's no hurry—and if you need help deciding what you want, just let me know."

The guy savored the martini and ambiance for a few minutes and then called the waiter over.

"Yes, sir, what may I do for you?"

"I'd like to start with escargots and then have the New York strip steak."

"Yes, sir. Fine choice. How would you like your steak?"

"Rare to medium rare. Dark pink."

"Dark pink it is!" said the waiter.

The escargots appetizer was on a par with the Paul Bocuse Restaurant in Lyon.

The waiter cleared away the appetizer dish and brought the main course on a large dinner plate covered with a silver dome. With a flourish he removed the dome and revealed a dreadful little overcooked hunk of beef that looked like shoe leather. It looked as tough as the rubber on an L.L. Bean Maine boot. It was disgusting and tasted awful.

He called the waiter over.

"Yes, sir, what may I do for you?" he asked, smiling broadly

"This steak is terrible—an embarrassment! Overcooked and tough as nails. You take this back to the chef and tell him to shove it up his ass."

"Yes, sir. Absolutely, sir. I'll be happy to!"

The offending plate was whisked away, and the waiter disappeared.

At length the salesman spotted the waiter across the room and motioned him over.

"Yes, sir. What may I do for you?"

"Did you tell the chef to shove that steak up his ass?"

"Absolutely, your exact words, sir."

"And what happened?"

"He said there was a lobster and two pressed ducks ahead of you."

Upmarket Restaurant #2

49. A couple went to one of New York's premier restaurants, La Grenouille, to celebrate their thirtieth wedding anniversary. The main dining room was full, and everyone was having a wonderful time with divine cuisine and great wines.

At the far side of the room was a table where two tuxedo-clad guys were drinking and getting louder and louder.

One of the young men got into conversation with a foursome at the adjoining table. He loudly boasted that he could take a sip of any wine in the world and identify the country, the vineyard, and the year.

One of the four patrons at the adjoining table passed a glass of red over to him and said, "Okay, I'll test you. Try this."

The young man sniffed the bouquet and then took a sip. "It's a Chateauneuf de Pape, vintage 2003."

"That's amazing!" the diner said.

From a table on the other side, a diner handed him a glass of white wine, and the guy said, "Ah, Saint Cyr, 2015."

"Incredible!" said the person at that table.

Soon everybody in the restaurant was proffering glasses of wine in an effort to trip up this wine expert, who was beginning to dominate all the conversation in the dining room. A number of patrons were irritated by the loud interruption. But the glasses of wine were coming fast and furious, and he was unerring in his identification.

Finally, a glass of pale-yellow white was passed to him. He took a sip, gagged, gulped some water, and cried, "That's awful! Yuck! It tastes like piss!"

"You got it!" shouted a guy from across the room. "What year was I born?"

50. Greek Restaurant

A Chinese gentleman and his wife and children were dining in a Greek restaurant. The big, burly Greek waiter came over and in a feigned Chinese accent said, "Ah, so you likee start with something to dlink?"

The adults ordered ouzos for themselves and ginger ales for the kids.

The waiter reappeared. "You likee Gleek food?"

In a cultured, clipped British accent, the Chinese patron said, "You should know I was born and brought up in England, attended Eton and Cambridge, and have a PhD from the London School of Economics. My entire family speaks perfect English, you Gleek plick!"

51. An Aussie Tale

The health inspectors raided a restaurant in Sydney, Australia.

The next day they returned. "We found horse meat in your rabbit stew."

"That can't be!" said the owner.

"Don't argue with us, mate. We've got proof."

The owner was silenced.

"How much horse meat was in the stew?" they demanded.

"Uh … uh … it was about fifty-fifty."

"What do you mean by fifty-fifty?"

"Uh … uh … one horse and one rabbit."

52. A Confusion of Newsmen

This is a story Walter Cronkite told on himself. In the 1960s and '70s, the lion of CBS News, Walter Cronkite, was frequently mistaken for Ron Cochran, a late-night anchor on WABC, a local New York City TV station. They did look alike, with pudgy faces and pencil-thin mustaches.

The confusion happened frequently on the street, and it irritated the hell out of Cronkite.

One day a woman stopped Cronkite on Fifth Avenue and excitedly said, "Oh my, Ron Cochran! I watch you every night, and I love your reporting. When you give the news, you are so believable and trustworthy. I just love you!" She paused and said, "You are Ron Cochran, aren't you?"

"Yes, madam, I'm Ron Cochran," Cronkite said. "Now fuck off."

53. The Ultimate Optimist

The child of a very wealthy couple was an incurable optimist. He was perpetually upbeat and frenetic and seemingly deranged. The kid was put into a program of psychoanalysis to try to calm him down, and he continued to be boisterous and happy.

"I'm afraid your son will grow up with a skewed personality," said the doctor. "Do you have a swimming pool?"

"Yes, we do."

"Fill it with horse manure, then toss him in and see what happens. This should bring him down to earth."

The pool was filled with truckloads of horse manure, and the kid put on a bathing suit and was pushed in.

He proceeded to jump in with gusto, splash around, dive in, come up for air, and dive back under in an explosion of pure happiness.

"What are you doing?" the parents wailed.

"There's got to be a pony somewhere in here!"

54. Poor Reception from the Moon

One evening astronaut Neil Armstrong was being interviewed for an early evening news program with Tom Brokaw. Armstrong—an authentic American hero—had just come from a reunion lunch with two astronaut buddies from his past and had drunk a tad more than he was used to.

Brokaw asked Armstrong how he had come up with the legendary phrase that had gripped the world: "One small step for a man, one giant leap for mankind."

"Actually, I have been misquoted all these years. My voice was not clear 250,000 miles from Earth. What I really said was 'One giant leap for Manny Klein.'"

"Oh, really?" exclaimed Brokaw, titillated at the possibility of making news. He changed the thrust of the program from a routine interview to a news story that would go around the world. "Who was Manny Klein?"

"Many years ago, shortly after I graduated from the academy, we were living in the MOQ—married officer's quarters—at the base. It was a low-budget building from World War II with cardboard walls. You could hear everything that was going on in the next apartment.

"Our neighbors were Sue and Manny Klein, and they argued a lot and got into shouting matches. As I said, you could hear every word."

"What happened?" Brokaw asked.

"An argument that started low and got louder and louder. Suddenly, Sue yelled, 'Manny Klein, I will give you a blow job the day man walks on the moon!'"

55. The Sci-Fi World

After traveling many years, six American astronauts arrived at a distant planet and found life! These were not human beings, but highly intelligent blob-like creatures with blob heads, blob bodies, four blob arms, and four blob legs.

The blobs spoke English, having eavesdropped on radio transmissions from Earth.

The astronauts and the blobs learned everything about each other—or almost everything—before the Americans were scheduled to return to Earth.

What was not understood: how did the blob people reproduce?

"Oh, it's very simple," a blob told them. The blob nodded to another blob, and they drew closer and closer until they joined.

A few seconds later, they separated, and on the ground between them was a teeny baby blob.

"Amazing!"

"How do humans make children?" the blobs asked.

The astronauts shuffled their feet and looked down in embarrassment.

"What's the matter?" the blob asked.

"Well … uh …"

"C'mon. We showed you. Now you show us."

The American captain said turnabout was fair play and ordered the female crew member to undress. The captain took off his space suit, and in the interest of science, the couple performed human intercourse.

They got up from their labors and were starting to put on their space suits when a blob asked, "Where is the human baby?"

"It doesn't come for nine months."

"Nine months? Not for nine months?"

"That's right, nine months."

"Then what was the rush at the end?"

56. Follow-Up to the Blob Joke

A eleven-year-old-kid was having his twelfth birthday later in the week.

"What do you want for your birthday?" the parents asked.

"I wanna watch."

So they let him.

57. An Eventful Flight to Chicago

In 1949 at New York's La Guardia Airport, a well-dressed young woman had just sat down in her aisle seat in a tiny, cramped Douglas DC-3, the noisy little two-engine airliner that every airline flew after the war. She was reading a book. At the last minute a handsome, elegant young man in a beautifully tailored blue suit with a yellow tie and matching yellow silk handkerchief in the breast pocket appeared and stood in front of the young woman.

"I believe I have the window seat," he said shyly with a warm smile.

She stood up, and he slipped by her to his window seat.

They chatted briefly, then he brought out a book from his briefcase, and they both read.

An hour into the uneventful flight, the young man suddenly clutched the airsickness bag from the seat pocket and held it in his mouth. With great difficulty in the tiny seat, he unbuckled his belt, unzipped his fly, wriggled out of his trousers and undershorts, and began grunting and groaning as he had a difficult bowel movement into the barf bag. When finished, he plucked the yellow silk handkerchief from his breast pocket, cleaned himself up, put the soiled handkerchief in the little bag, folded and sealed it, and returned the bag to the seat pocket. Then with great difficulty in the tiny space, he pulled up his shorts and trousers, zipped the fly, buckled his seat belt, and returned to the book he was reading.

Fifteen minutes later, he turned to the young woman, smiled, and said shyly in a soft voice, "Do you mind if I smoke?"

58. Boris Thomashefsky (1866–1939)

The greatest actor of Yiddish theater (and grandfather of conductor Michael Tilson Thomas) adored women, and the adoration was reciprocal.

He was always elegantly dressed in tailored clothes, suede gloves, and evening capes. One evening he picked up a starlet who agreed to go to a hotel with him, where they had a riotous night of lovemaking.

The next morning, Thomashefsky got out of bed, got dressed, and started to leave. "Are you leaving without giving me some money?" she wailed.

"Money? Money? I'm a world-famous actor. I am Boris Thomashefsky. You should be flattered I even looked at you!"

"But I have no money!"

"I'm an actor! I give away passes, not money."

"But I am broke! I need to eat! I need bread!"

"Next time, fuck a baker!"

59. Boris Thomashefsky dropped dead in the middle of a play. Many in the audience screamed. The stage manager closed the curtain.

Moments later, the theater manager came through the curtains to the apron, and the audience went quiet.

"Ladies and gentlemen, terrible news. The great voice of Thomashefsky is silenced forever."

A woman in the balcony shouted, "Give 'im an enema!"

"Madam, Thomashefsky is no more!"

"Give 'im an enema!

"But he is dead! An enema won't do any good!"

"So it can't hurt!"

60. Upmarket Golf Resort

The golf resort and spa had a fantastic reputation for its accommodations, the quality of its fairways and greens, the great bar, and its superb cuisine.

A very wealthy mogul heard about it, checked in, and was dazzled. The room rate was very inexpensive. The bar tab was a tiny amount. Dinner and breakfast were sumptuous and included with the room.

After breakfast he went into the golf pro shop and asked to rent a set of clubs. The pro produced a gorgeous new bag with a complete set of Callaway Epic clubs.

"How much to rent these?" the man asked.

"They're on the house," the pro said. "No charge."

"No charge? Really? That's unbelievable!"

"Happy to oblige."

"Let me have a dozen balls."

The pro produced twelve custom Titleist golf balls. "That'll be $1,500 each—$18,000.00—charged to your account."

"Twelve golf balls! Eighteen thousand dollars! That's outrageous! Everything else is so cheap! What's going on?"

"Anywhere else you go, they'll get you by the rooms."

61. Multiple Marriages

True story: My former boss, Jack Barlass, book salesman and book publisher (*Better Homes and Gardens* plaid cookbook), was a rough and gruff guy who liked hanging out with guys at the New York Athletic Club and drinking. His wife, Florelle, was a tiny, very sweet woman who died after a long bout with Alzheimer's. Jack surprised everyone by going into deep grief—real, deep grief to the point where he sought counseling.

After a full year of solitary living in a Florida retirement community, Jack, on the advice of his grief counselor, decided to attend his first social function at a neighbor's home. He got duded up in his best outfit, put a bottle of good wine in a gift bag, and rang the neighbor's doorbell.

The hostess opened the door, and Jack said, "I'm Jack Barlass."

The woman stepped back and said, "My gosh, you look just like my third husband!"

"Uh … how many times have you been married?" Jack asked.

"Twice."

62. Quizzo True Story

During a very boozy Quizzo evening at the East Hampton home of our great friend and fellow Players member actor Peter Turgeon, everyone was blotto. The Quizzo question was: "What was the name of General Robert E. Lee's horse?"

"I give up. What was the name of Robert E. Lee's horse?"

"C'mon, guess."

"Give me a hint."

"A hint, okay. Think of an insurance company."

"Mutual of Omaha!"

(Lee's horse was Traveler.)

63. J.P. Morgan Story (True)

In the nineteenth century, the most powerful financier in the world was J.P. Morgan, a hulking man with massive shoulders, piercing eyes, and a freakish, bulbous purple nose, the result of rosacea, a chronic skin disease. Consumed by self-consciousness about his nose, he despised being photographed and hated publicity. All photographs of him were ordered retouched.

Shortly before his death in 1913, Morgan was invited to tea by Morgan partner Dwight Morrow and his wife Elizabeth. Their daughter, Anne Morrow (later Mrs. Charles Lindbergh), was seven years old and was going to be presented to Mr. Morgan. Anne's mother was terrified that the moppet would stare at Morgan's nose and maybe say something. Elizabeth Morrow explained to Anne that Mr. Morgan had this nose condition and cautioned her not to say anything about it. "Don't look. Pretend it's not there."

Morgan arrived, and little Anne curtsied when presented to the great man. She then gawked at his nose, her eyes bulging and mouth open.

The Morrows were horrified. Finally, Anne was dismissed and left the room.

Mrs. Morrow poured a cup of tea for the financier and said, "Mr. Morgan, would like some sugar and cream in your nose?"

64. Danger in Africa

A recently retired couple was in Rwanda on a photographic safari when the wife was grabbed by a huge male gorilla, who picked her up and disappeared with her deep into the woods as she screamed. An all-points bulletin was issued, and three weeks later, the Rwandan military found the woman in a cave and brought her back to civilization. At first, she was glassy-eyed and silent, and then she started wailing and crying. She wept and cried all the way back to the US on the plane. Once home, she took to her bed, sobbing pitifully. The tears went on for a week. She was so deeply affected by the experience that she was incapable of talking or communicating.

After a month of sobbing, not eating, and being incapable of communicating, the family doctor recommended a counselor who was world renowned in dealing with women's emotional trauma.

In the counselor's private office, she broke down and started wailing piteously.

Handing the distraught woman a Kleenex, the counselor said, "The only way to get this behind us is to talk it through. Could you do that with me? Tell me what you are thinking?"

The woman burst into violent sobs and said, "He doesn't phone. He doesn't write!"

65. Celestial Game of Golf

God and St. Peter are at the first tee of the great Celestial Golf Course.

St. Peter tees up his ball, takes a couple of practice strokes, and then whacks his ball right down the middle of the first fairway with a memorable drive.

God then steps up and wildly mishits the ball, which hooks way to the right, into the long grass of the rough.

As they start trudging down the fairway, a squirrel suddenly pops out of the woods, grabs God's ball in its mouth, and starts running in the opposite direction.

A giant eagle circling above then swoops down and grabs the squirrel (with God's ball still in its mouth) and starts flying over the fairway toward the first hole.

When the eagle and squirrel are over the first green, the eagle's talons squeeze the squirrel, who disgorges God's ball, which lands on the green and rolls slowly into the cup.

A hole in one for God!

"Okay," says St. Peter. "Are you here to play golf or just screw around?"

66. An Academic Brouhaha

A world-renowned professor of electronics at Notre Dame University boarded the New York Central *Lake Shore Limited* in South Bend, Indiana.

Before going into the dining car for dinner, he buttonholed the African American porter in charge of his Pullman sleeper car and told him he had an important meeting the following day with scientists at General Electric. That meant he had to wake up at 4:15 a.m. and get off the train at 4:45 a.m. in Schenectady, New York. It was a hugely important meeting that could result in a massive consulting project, and he could not miss it.

The porter nodded. "I won't let you miss the stop, sir," the porter said.

The professor explained to the porter that he was a very deep sleeper and had a hard time waking up. "If you try to wake me up from a deep sleep, I can get nasty," the traveler said. "It's not your fault; it's mine. But I can start screaming at you and pushing you away, refusing to get up. As I say, it's not your fault. But whatever I say, don't let me miss that stop!"

"I won't, sir. I promise."

The professor handed the porter a twenty-dollar bill.

"Why, thank you, sir."

After a fine dinner and a surprisingly good bottle of wine, the professor went to bed in his compartment.

The next thing he heard was the loudspeaker throughout the train: "Attention, passengers: this stop is Poughkeepsie, New York. We will reach New York City in one hour and a half. Thank you."

The professor sat bolt upright and went nuts. He rang for the porter and started to shave. The porter rapped on the door, and the professor snarled for him to come in. The porter entered, and the professor proceeded to rip him up and down for not getting him off the train at Schenectady. He demanded that the conductor phone ahead to get a senior railroad official to meet the train along with the porter's boss at the next station.

The professor screamed at the porter and conductor all the way to New York. After detraining, he continued yelling at the railroad VP and the porter's boss on the platform. Meanwhile, the railroad had a limousine and chauffeur ready to drive him to Schenectady so he would not be that late for the meeting. The professor—still screaming and raging about what had happened—marched through the station to the limo, followed by the porter, railroad official, and train conductor. He got in and drove off.

The railroad VP turned to the old porter and said, "Sam, I have never seen a man that angry. He is the maddest man I have ever seen!"

"Pardon me, boss," said the porter. "But if you think he was mad, you should have seen the guy I put off the train at Schenectady."

67. The Perfect Squelch

For twenty years we lived in a row house on a little street in Philadelphia. Three times during the summer—Memorial Day, July Fourth and Labor Day—we celebrated with a block party. A long table was set in the middle of the street and all the neighbors brought out wonderful food (including a traditional roast pig on Independence Day) along with chilled wine and ice-cold beer. There were games and a wading pool for the children. Friends and family from the neighborhood and the suburbs came by enjoy the festivities.

On one occasion I was with three other people whom I had never met. Opposite me was Dr. Bruce Jones and two women who proceeded to dominate the conversation nattering on about their children while Bruce and I listened in awkward silence. Realizing the two men were being left out, one of the ladies turned to me and asked, "Do you have children, Mr. Hatch."

I replied, "No ma'am. In three marriages I never had children. I wake up every morning and thank God I'm sterile."

Whereupon Bruce—without missing a beat—said, "Denny, everybody in Philadelphia thanks God you're sterile!"

68. A Pickup Attempt

A very short guy walks into a bar, and on a bar stool facing the entrance sits a gorgeous young blonde woman with long legs and a short skirt.

The short man swaggers up to her and says, "What would you say to a little fuck?"

"I'd say, 'Hello, little fuck.'"

69. If Doggies Do It …

Every weekday morning, George would start walking down the sidewalk, and at the next block he would meet up with Harry. They would walk the remaining three blocks to the commuter train and ride to work. One morning they encountered two dogs having sex on a neighbor's lawn.

"If you haven't tried it that way," said Harry, "it's really great."

"Huh? Whaddya talking about?"

"Sex. Doggy style. It's terrific. Give it a try. You'll both love it!"

"Really?"

"Promise."

The next morning, George picked up Harry. "We did it," George said.

"Did what?"

"Did it doggy style."

"Was it as good as I said it would be?"

"It was terrific! It took four martinis before she agreed to it."

"Four martinis! What happened?"

"It took three martinis to get her out on the lawn."

70. A Strange Illness to Tell the Queen About

Her Majesty the Queen visited wounded warriors in a military hospital in London during the Falklands War. She slowly went through the ward, chatting up the horribly wounded troops who were in splints and covered with bandages.

At one bed there was a trooper with no bandages and no splints who looked perfectly healthy.

"You look wonderful," the queen said. "What seems to be the problem?"

"Boils on me bum, Mum."

Her Majesty muttered how sorry she was and moved on.

The queen left the building, and everybody in the place went ballistic. How could this clot say such a thing to the queen! It was hugely embarrassing. "Never say a thing like that again!" the aghast staff yammered at the poor guy.

Two days later, Her Royal Highness Anne, the Princess Royal, came through the ward. She passed this same trooper's bed and asked what the problem was.

"Boils … boils, uh … boils on me … *on me back*, Mum."

"Oh, Mother will be so sorry to hear they've spread."

Two Castration Stories

71. A Strange, Very Rare Illness

A well-to-do man in his late thirties suddenly developed a terrible, painful ringing in his ears and horrific migraine headaches that seemed to take over his whole body. He was desperate, unable to concentrate at work and sleep-deprived. He checked into a hospital for tests.

After extensive examinations by specialists in many fields, the doctors traced the ringing sound plus migraines to some kind of rare abnormality in his testicles.

"Oh my God! What's the treatment?"

"The only sure cure is castration."

"C-c-c-c-castration?"

"I'm afraid so."

The guy refused. But the ringing, the migraine pain, and the sleep deprivation got worse, to the point where he could not function. Finally, he agreed to the operation for the sake of his sanity. The operation went off without a hitch, and he was cured!

But he went into a deep depression about the loss of his manhood and sought psychiatric help. At one point his shrink suggested he do something to cheer himself up. For example, go to Boyd's—the leading menswear store in town—and treat himself to a completely new wardrobe, toes to nose, inside and out.

He went to Boyd's and was greeted by the top salesman, who eyeballed him and started making notes. "Size 44 suit. Sleeves twenty-seven inches. Waist forty. Inseam thirty-one inches." When the tailor measured him, the salesman's estimates proved to be absolutely spot-on.

The guy bought two new suits, a blue blazer, and two extra pairs of trousers.

In the shirt department, the salesman said, "Collar seventeen inches, sleeves twenty-seven inches." Again absolutely correct. The guy was feeling better than he had in days.

In the underwear department the salesman said, "Medium T-shirts and Jockey briefs with a forty-inch waist."

"No!" the guy said. "I always get a thirty-six-inch waist!"

"Forty!" the sales rep snapped.

"Thirty-six," said the customer.

"Don't do it!" the salesman insisted. "Thirty-six waist is too tight. They'll crimp your balls and cause terrible migraines and ringing in the ears!"

72. A Shaggy Horse Story

A very promising, very fast two-year-old racehorse kept acting up at the starting gate. The result: late starts, dazzling speed, but lost races. The owner and trainer decided the only solution was to geld him.

The deed was done. In his first start as a gelding, he seemed totally at ease. When the starting gate sprang open, he tore out onto the course into the immediate lead. Suddenly, he tripped and fell, and five horses piled up on top of him. It was a mess.

Back in the barn, the winning horse asked him, "What the hell happened to you?"

"I was feeling great. Got a great start. Suddenly, the track announcer yelled, 'They're off!' and I got so embarrassed I crossed my legs."

73. A Fabulous Jewel

A stunning older woman arrived at a white-tie dinner party in Beverly Hills. She wore a glorious, tight-fitting, azure full-length ball gown that showed off her remarkable figure. She sported an eye-popping, heart-stopping necklace with a thirty-two-carat diamond pendant resting at the top of her ample cleavage.

"My God! What a beautiful diamond!" a handsome older gentleman exulted. "I don't think I've seen anything like it in my life."

"It's the ten-million-dollar Plotkin diamond," she said. "It is beautiful, but it comes with a terrible curse."

"What kind of a curse?" he asked.

"Harvey Plotkin."

Two Men's Room Stories—Both Visual
(Acted out in the telling)

74. The Perils of Being Famous

(This is told from the point of view of the guy standing at the next urinal.)

In the early 1990s came the sad news that beloved American actor James (Jimmy) Stewart was reported to be ill and unable to appear in public. The scuttlebutt was that he had had an embarrassing bout of incontinence at Sardi's restaurant in New York City's Theater District.

Stewart was seen walking through the main dining room to his table from a quick trip to the second-floor men's room. His pants were soaking wet. The waiter quickly appeared and spread two cloth napkins across Stewart's lap.

The backstory: Stewart had been standing at the urinal next to a tourist, who looked to his left, noticed the famous actor, did a double-take, and realized it was indeed the Hollywood legend next to him.

Still urinating, the guy turned to face Stewart, threw up his hands, and—as he pissed all over the great star—exclaimed, "My God, you're Jimmy Stewart!"

75. Mistaken for a Korean Veteran

(The teller of this story must be wearing a jacket or sweater with his hands concealed under the sleeves, so that he appears to be a double amputee.)

A guy walked into a men's room and found a man with no hands standing by the urinal.

"I need help," the man said.

"Of course," said the other man. He reached over and unzipped the luckless gentleman's fly and helped him urinate. When the man was finished, the helper gave the guy's limb a gentle shake and then zipped up his fly.

"Thank you, thank you," the guy said.

"What happened? Was it Korea?"

The guy's hands miraculously reappeared out of his sleeves. "Gonorrhea. I don't dare touch the filthy thing."

76. A Foreign Accent Problem

At a holiday party of millennials in cosmopolitan San Francisco, an exotic, beautiful young girl arrived—a recent immigrant from a Middle Eastern country who had just celebrated her eighteenth birthday. Stunning to look at in her bright patterned sari, she was very innocent and very shy and was struggling with her English, which she spoke with a very pronounced foreign accent.

An equally shy and very rich millennial young man was dazzled, and he monopolized her for the evening. They dated, he proposed marriage, and six weeks later, they eloped.

Upon their return from their honeymoon, they attended a big party in their honor. Everyone asked the new bride how she like being married.

"Oh," she said, "wonderful! Such a penis!"

"What?"

"Such a penis!"

All who overheard the exchange were aghast. Word of her gaffe was repeated throughout the party.

Finally, a girlfriend she had grown up with, who had come to the US as a child and spoke perfect English, explained to her what she had said. The poor girl was mortified. They had a long whispered conversation.

All eyes were on the friend, who said to the crowd, "What she means is 'such *happiness*'!"

77. Two Very Old Guys Compare Notes

When very senior men marry very young trophy wives, all is not always simpatico. Two very rich geezers in their eighties had each recently wed much, much younger women. They bumped into each other at their men's club, and Geezer #1 said, "Been meaning to ask you, old chap, about how you're handling physical relations with that young minx you married."

"I got the same question for you," said Geezer #2, "the question of this sex business."

"Tri-weekly," said Geezer #1.

"Tri-weekly! That's amazing! Exactly the same with me! What a coincidence!"

"By the way, how are you spelling 'tri'?"

"How do you spell 'weekly'?"

78. Three Deaf Brits

Three very deaf old Englishmen were in the club car of a train as it pulled into a station.

"I say, what stop is this?" asked Geezer #1.

"It's Wembley," said Geezer #2.

"Wembley? I thought it was Thursday," said Geezer #3.

"So am I," said Geezer #1. "Let's have a drink!"

79. When the Weather Is Frigid

The year was 1951, and it was a cold, icy, snowy day. Two young women were waiting for a bus. One of the women was wearing a short quilted coat and traditional nylon stockings. She was obviously very cold. She noticed that the other woman was wearing warm black tights and asked where she'd gotten them.

"This is a leotard," she said. "Dancers wear them to keep their legs warm."

"How high up do they go?"

"They go all the way up. They keep my hips and rear end warm. They keep my thighs warm. They keep my legs and ankles warm, and they keep my feet warm. I love them!"

"Is there anything you don't like about them?"

"Yeah, every time I fart, I blow my shoes off."

80. Definition of Three Great Religions

A rabbi, a Protestant minister, and a Catholic priest were discussing their basic beliefs.

Rabbi: "We take care of people from the cradle to the grave."

Protestant minister: "Our flock can count on us from the tomb of the womb to the womb of the tomb."

Catholic priest: "Our promise: from erection to resurrection."

81. In the 1980s and '90s, my wife Peggy was an official in the World Curling Federation, and we did some international travel to various places in Europe. One day in Grindelwald, Germany, I was waiting in the hotel bar while Peggy was in a session when a tall Swedish curler named Per wandered in. He was a lovely guy, very affable, although I had never thought he had much sense of humor. "Can I buy you beer?" I asked him. "It's going to be a hearty, dense German beer," I said, "none of the weak and tasteless American variety."

"American beer is like making love in a canoe," said Per.

"What do you mean?"

"It's fucking close to water."

82. Meeting Sammy Davis Jr.

A member at the swanky Wingfoot Country Club in Westchester County just north of New York walked into the dining rooms. Seated at the bar was a lone guy who looked just like Sammy Davis Jr. The member stopped and gawked. He had seen the great entertainer just the week before in Las Vegas, creating mayhem with the Rat Pack—Frank Sinatra, Dean Martin, Johnny Carson, and Joey Bishop.

"My gosh!" he said. "You look just like Sammy Davis Jr."

"That's me. Hi there."

"I had no idea you play golf … gee, what's your handicap?"

"My handicap?" Davis said. "You're asking a one-eyed black Jew!"

83. The World's Shortest Joke (Nine Words)

He: Do you smoke after intercourse?
She: Dunno. I never looked.

The Joy of Limericks

Note: Limericks are happy—usually raunchy—little poems that reportedly go back to the thirteenth century, the first one being penned in Latin by Saint Thomas Aquinas (1225–74). It had to do with—what else?—sex. The second line calls for the "extermination of lust." Here is the Thomas Aquinas original (in Latin) followed by my favorite three limericks. Think of them as mini-patter songs sans music.

84.

Sit vitiorum meorum evacuatio

Concupiscentae et libidinis exterminatio,

Caritatis et patientiae,

Humilitatis et obedientiae,

Omniumque virtutum augmentatio

85.

The limerick packs laughs anatomical
Into space that is quite economical.
But the good ones I've seen
So seldom are clean
And the clean ones so seldom are comical.
—Unknown

86.

Note: The story has it that the following limerick was created by that Victorian master of nonsense Edward Lear (1812–88) on a bet. Someone bet Lear a large sum of money that he could not make a rhyme of the English town of Aberystwyth. Lear won the bet.

There was a young girl from Aberystwyth
Who took grain to the mill to make grist with
When a miller named Jack
Put her flat on her back
And they mingled the organs they pissed with.
—Edward Lear

87.

As Titian was mixing rose attar
His model was nude on a ladder
Her position to Titian
Suggested coition
So he climbed up the ladder and had her.

Part 3

SIXTEEN LEGENDARY ENGLISH-LANGUAGE PATTER SONGS (1875–1917)

Note: In the e-book edition of *Bawdy Jokes and Patter Songs*, for each of these seventy-eight patter songs, I have included the following links:

In Performance: Click on the YouTube link and delight in seeing and hearing the songs as interpreted by the greatest entertainers of yesteryear and today.

Actual Full Lyrics: The sixteen famous early patter songs are pre-1926. Copyright protection has expired, and I am allowed to print their lyrics since they are in the public domain. Full lyrics accompany each of these songs.

Google Links to Lyrics of Modern Patter Songs: The seventy-one modern patter songs are under copyright protection and cannot be printed without permission. These lyrics are found on myriad websites, and Google key words have been provided to help you locate them.

Note: There are commercials and ads. YouTube deserves income, hence the short commercials. They last but a few seconds.

Sixteen Famous Early Patter Songs

ABOUT GILBERT AND SULLIVAN

Sir William Schwenck Gilbert (1836–1911)
Sir Arthur Sullivan (1842–1900)

Born in London, Schwenck Gilbert started out as a multifaceted playwright-librettist-poet-illustrator-cartoonist-essayist with a delicious sense of humor and an incredible command of the English language. He came up with the concept of "topsy-turvy," whereby he creates an absurd situation that results in a series of logical follow-ups until everything is happily resolved.

In 1870 Gilbert was introduced to composer Arthur Sullivan by theatrical impresario Richard D'Oyly Carte, and they all began working together. Their first hit was *H.M.S. Pinafore* in 1878, and it ran for a boffo 578 performances. The leading character, Sir Joseph Porter, KCB, was a send-up of real-life bookseller and news agent William Henry Smith (1825–91). A member of the ubiquitous British bookstore family of W. H. Smith, he was elected to Parliament in 1866 and was appointed First Lord of the Admiralty in 1877 by Prime Minister Benjamin Disraeli. Thereafter he was forever known as "Pinafore Smith."

The twenty-five-year collaboration made topsy-turvy hash of historical events. But all was not smooth sailing for the *Pinafore* pair. Sullivan disdained writing music for lowbrow comic operas. Rather, he yearned to do serious composing. But the D'Oyly Carte Opera Company was a cash cow that enabled Gilbert and Sullivan to live the high life. They created fourteen operettas, many of which are regularly performed throughout the world after nearly 150 years and will be delighting audiences for many years to come.

Note: If you want a terrific bio-picture of Gilbert and Sullivan, rent Mike Leigh's delicious *Topsy-Turvy* (2000). It's available free on YouTube. "Set in the 1880s, the story of how, during a creative dry spell, the partnership of the legendary musical/theatrical writers Gilbert and Sullivan almost dissolves, before they turn it all around and write *The Mikado*" (IMDB).

Gilbert and Sullivan
Trial by Jury (1875), 131 performances
1. "When I, Good Friends, Was Called to the Bar"

IN PERFORMANCE: ANTHONY WARLOW
https://www.youtube.com/watch?v=R_Muda8caMQ
YouTube Key Words:
When I good friends was called to the bar Warlow

FULL LYRICS:
[Judge]
When I, good friends, was call'd to the bar
I'd an appetite fresh and hearty
But I was, as many young barristers are
An impecunious party
I'd a swallow-tail coat of a beautiful blue
And a brief which I bought of a booby
A couple of shirts, and a collar or two
And a ring that looked like a ruby

[Chorus]
He'd a couple of shirts, and a collar or two
And a ring that look'd like a ruby

[Judge]
At Westminister Hall I danc'd a dance
Like a semi-despondent fury
For I tho't I never should hit on a chance
Of addressing a British jury
But I soon got tired of third-class journeys
And dinners of bread and water
So I fell in love with a rich attorney's
Elderly, ugly daughter

[Chorus]
So he fell in love with a rich attorney's
Elderly, ugly daughter

[Judge]

The rich attorney, he jump'd with joy
And replied to my fond professions
"You shall reap the reward of your pluck, my boy
At the Bailey and Middlesex Sessions
You'll soon get used to her looks," said he
"And a very nice girl you will find her
She may very well pass for forty-three
In the dusk, with a light behind her"

[Chorus]

She has often been taken for forty-three
In the dusk, with a light behind her

[Judge]

The rich attorney was good as his word
The briefs came trooping gaily
And every day my voice was heard
At the Sessions of ancient Bailey
All thieves, who could my fees afford
Relied on my orations
And many a burglar I've restored
To his friends and his relations

[Chorus]

And many a burglar he's restored
To his friends and his relations

[Judge]

At length I became as rich as the Gurneys
An incubus then I thought her
So I threw over that rich attorney's
Elderly, ugly daughter
The rich attorney my character high
Tried vainly to disparage
And now, if you please, I'm ready to try
This breach of promise of marriage

[Chorus]
And now, if you please, he's ready to try
This breach of promise of marriage

[Judge]
For now I'm a judge

[Chorus]
And a good judge, too

[Judge]
Yes, now I'm a judge

[Chorus]
And a good judge, too

[Judge]
Though all my law be fudge
Yet I'll never, never budge
And I'll live and die a judge

[Chorus]
And a good judge too

[Judge]
It was managed by a job—
And a good job, too!
It was managed by a job!
And a good job too!
It is patent to the mob,
That my being made a nob
Was effected by a job.
And a good job too!

—W. S. Gilbert (1875)

Gilbert and Sullivan
The Sorcerer (1877), 178 performances
2. "My Name Is John Wellington Wells"

IN PERFORMANCE: MARTYN GREEN
https://www.youtube.com/watch?v=6sLdkLXY9Is&t=3s
YouTube Key Words:
Martyn Green the Sorcerer

FULL LYRICS:
Oh, my name is John Wellington Wells
I'm a dealer in magic and spells
In blessings and curses
And ever-filled purses
In prophecies, witches, and knells
If you want a proud foe to "make tracks"
If you'd melt a rich uncle in wax
You've but to look in on our resident Djinn
Number seventy, Simmery Axe
We've a first-class assortment of magic
And for raising a posthumous shade
With effects that are comic or tragic
There's no cheaper house in the trade
Love-philtre, we've quantities of it
And for knowledge if any one burns
We keep an extremely small prophet, a prophet
Who brings us unbounded returns
For he can prophesy with a wink of his eye
Peep with security into futurity
Sum up your history, clear up a mystery
Humor proclivity for a nativity
He has answers oracular, bogies spectacular
Tetrapods tragical, mirrors so magical
Facts astronomical, solemn or comical
And, if you want it, he
Makes a reduction on taking a quantity
Oh, if any one anything lacks
He'll find it all ready in stacks
If he'll only look in on the resident Djinn

Number seventy, Simmery Axe
He can raise you hosts of ghosts
And that without reflectors
And creepy things with wings
And gaunt and grisly spectres
He can fill you crowds of shrouds
And horrify you vastly
He can rack your brains with chains
And gibberings grim and ghastly
Then, if you plan it, he changes organity
With an urbanity full of Satanity
Vexing humanity with an inanity
Fatal to vanity
Driving your foes to the verge of insanity
But in tautology on demonology
'Lectro biology, mystic nosology
Spirit philology, high class astrology
Such is his knowledge, he
Isn't the man to require an apology
Oh, my name is John Wellington Wells
I'm a dealer in magic and spells
In blessings and curses
And ever-filled purses
In prophecies, witches, and knells
If anyone anything lacks
He'll find it all ready in stacks
If he'll only look in on the resident Djinn
Number seventy, Simmery Axe

—W. S. Gilbert (1877)

Gilbert and Sullivan
H.M.S. Pinafore (1878), 571 performances
3. "I Am the Monarch of the Sea"/"When I Was a Lad"

IN PERFORMANCE: DREW FORSYTHE
https://www.youtube.com/watch?v=iZ-gfalEWI0
YouTube Key Words:
I am the Monarch of the Sea Forsythe

FULL LYRICS:

"I Am the Monarch of the Sea"

[Sir Joseph]
I am the monarch of the sea,
The ruler of the Queen's Navee,
Whose praise Great Britain loudly chants.

[Cousin Hebe]
And we are his sisters, and his cousins, and his aunts!

[All]
And we are his sisters, and his cousins, and his aunts!

[Sir Joseph]
When at anchor here I ride,
My bosom swells with pride,
And I snap my fingers at a foeman's taunts;

[Cousin Hebe]
And so do his sisters, and his cousins, and his aunts!

[All]
And so do his sisters, and his cousins, and his aunts!

[Sir Joseph]
But when the breezes blow,
I generally go below,
And seek the seclusion that a cabin grants;

[Cousin Hebe]

And so do his sisters, and his cousins, and his aunts!

[All]

And so do his sisters, and his cousins, and his aunts!
His sisters and his cousins, Whom he reckons up by dozens, And his aunts!

"When I Was a Lad"

[Sir Joseph]

When I was a lad I served a term
As office boy to an Attorney's firm.
I cleaned the windows and I swept the floor,
And I polished up the handle of the big front door.

[All]

He polished up the handle of the big front door.

[Sir Joseph]

I polished up that handle so carefully
That now I am the Ruler of the Queen's Navy!

[All]

He polished up that handle so carefullee,
That now he is the ruler of the Queen's Navee!

[Sir Joseph]

As office boy I made such a mark
That they gave me the post of a junior clerk.
I served the writs with a smile so bland,
And I copied all the letters in a big round hand.

[All]

He copied all the letters in a big round hand.

[Sir Joseph]

I copied all the letters in a hand so free,
That now I am the Ruler of the Queen's Navee!

[All]

He copied all the letters in a hand so free
That now he is the Ruler of the Queen's Navee!

[Sir Joseph]

In serving writs I made such a name
That an articled clerk I soon became;
I wore clean collars and a brand-new suit
For the passed examination at the Institute

[All]

For the passed examination at the Institute.

[Sir Joseph]

That passed examination did so well for me,
That now I am the Ruler of the Queen's Navee!

[All]

That passed examination did so well for he,
That now he is the Ruler of the Queen's Navee!

[Sir Joseph]

Of legal knowledge I acquired such a grip
That they took me into partnership.
The Junior Partnership I wean
Is the only ship I ever had seen!

[All]

Is the only ship he ever had seen.

[Sir Joseph]

That kind of ship so suited me
That now I am the Ruler of the Queen's Navy!

[All]

But that kind of ship so suited he
That now he is the ruler of Queen's Navee!

[Sir Joseph]

I grew so rich that I was sent

By a pocket borough into Parliament.
I always voted to my party's call
And I never thought of thinking for myself at all.

[All]

He never thought of thinking for himself at all!

[Sir Joseph]

I thought so little they rewarded me
By making me the Ruler of the Queen's Navee!

[All]

He thought so little they rewarded he
By making me the Ruler of the Queen's Navee!

[Sir Joseph]

Now landsmen all if whoever you may be
If you want to rise to the top of the tree
If your soul isn't fetters to an office stool,
Be careful to be guided by the Golden Rule.
Stick close to your desks and never go to sea
And you all may be Rulers of the Queen's Navee!

[All]

Stick close to your desks and never go to sea
And you all may be Rulers of the Queen's Navee!

—W. S. Gilbert (1878)

Gilbert and Sullivan
The Pirates of Penzance (1879), 363 performances
4. "I Am the Very Model of a Modern Major-General"

IN PERFORMANCE: MARTYN GREEN
https://www.youtube.com/watch?v=NpQyrDSrYIY
YouTube Key Words:
Major-General's Song Martyn Green

IN PERFORMANCE: GEORGE ROSE

https://www.youtube.com/watch?v=lC8Z8j4evpY

YouTube Key Words:

Major General George Rose

FULL LYRICS:

[Major-General]

I am the very model of a modern Major-General,

I've information vegetable, animal, and mineral,

I know the kings of England, and I quote the fights historical

From Marathon to Waterloo, in order categorical;

I'm very well acquainted, too, with matters mathematical,

I understand equations, both the simple and quadratical,

About binomial theorem I'm teeming with a lot o' news,

Hmmm … lot o' news, lot o'news … Aha!

With many cheerful facts about the square of the hypotenuse.

I'm very good at integral and differential calculus;

I know the scientific names of beings animalculous:

In short, in matters vegetable, animal, and mineral,

I am the very model of a modern Major-General.

I know our mythic history, King Arthur's and Sir Caradoc's;

I answer hard acrostics, I've a pretty taste for paradox,

I quote in elegiacs all the crimes of Heliogabalus,

In conics I can floor peculiarities parabolous;

I can tell undoubted Raphaels from Gerard Dows and Zoffanies,

I know the croaking from the Frogs of Aristophanes!

Then I can hum a fugue of which I've heard the music's din afore,

Hmmm … din afore, din afore … Aha!

And whistle all the airs from that infernal nonsense Pinafore.

Then I can write a washing bill in Babylonic cuneiform,

And tell you ev'ry detail of Caractacus's uniform:

In short, in matters vegetable, animal, and mineral,

I am the very model of a modern Major-General.

In fact, when I know what is meant by "mamelon" and "ravelin,"

When I can tell at sight a Mauser rifle from a javelin,

When such affairs as sorties and surprises I'm more wary at,

And when I know precisely what is meant by "commissariat,"

When I have learnt what progress has been made in modern gunnery,

When I know more of tactics than a novice in a nunnery

In short, when I've a smattering of elemental strategy

Hmmm … strategy … strategy, lategy, bategy … Aha! I have it!

You'll say a better Major-General has never sat a gee.

For my military knowledge, though I'm plucky and adventury,

Has only been brought down to the beginning of the century;

But still, in matters vegetable, animal, and mineral,

I am the very model of a modern Major-General.

—W. S. Gilbert (1879)

Gilbert and Sullivan
Patience **(1881), 578 performances**
5. "When I Go Out of Door"

IN PERFORMANCE: DAVE ROSS AND JOHN BROOKES
https://www.youtube.com/watch?v=K24iQwzPX9c
YouTube Key Words:
Seattle G&S: when I go out of door

FULL LYRICS:
[Bunthorne]
When I go out of door,
Of damozels a score
(All sighing and burning,
And clinging and yearning)
Will follow me as before.
I shall, with cultured taste,
Distinguish gems from paste,
And "High diddle diddle"
Will rank as an idyll,
If I pronounce it chaste!

[Both]
A most intense young man,
A soulful-eyed young man,
An ultra-poetical, super-aesthetical,
Out-of-the-way young man!

[Grosvenor]

Conceive me, if you can,
An ev'ryday young man:
A commonplace type,
With a stick and a pipe,
And a half-bred black-and-tan;
Who thinks suburban "hops"
More fun than "Monday Pops,"
Who's fond of his dinner,
And doesn't get thinner
On bottled beer and chops.

[Both]

A commonplace young man,
A matter-of-fact young man,
A steady and stolid-y, jolly Bank-holiday,
Every-day young man!

[Bunthorne]

A Japanese young man,
A blue-and-white young man,
Francesca di Rimini, miminy, piminy,
Je-ne-sais-quoi young man!

[Grosvenor]

A Chancery lane young man,
A Somerset House young man,
A very delectable, highly respectable,
Threepenny-bus young man!

[Bunthorne]

A pallid and thin young man,
A haggard and lank young man,
A greenery-yallery, Grosvenor Gallery,
Foot-in-the-grave young man!

[Grosvenor]

A Sewell and Cross young man,
A Howell and James young man,

A pushing young particle—
"What's the next article?"—
Waterloo House young man!

[Bunthorne] [Grosvenor]
Conceive me, if you can, Conceive me, if you can,
A crotchety, cracked young man, A matter-of-fact young man,
An ultra-poetical, super-aesthetical, An alphabetical, arithmetical,
Out-of-the-way young man! Every-day young man!

—W. S. Gilbert (1881)

Gilbert and Sullivan
Patience **(1881), 578 performances**
6. "If You're Anxious for to Shine"

IN PERFORMANCE: DANNY KAYE
https://www.youtube.com/results?search_query=If+you're+anxious+Danny+Kaye
YouTube Key Words:
If you're anxious Danny Kaye

FULL LYRICS:
[Bunthorne]
If you're anxious for to shine in the high aesthetic line
as a man of culture rare,
You must get up all the germs of the transcendental terms,
and plant them ev'rywhere.
You must lie upon the daisies and discourse in novel phrases
of your complicated state of mind,
The meaning doesn't matter if it's only idle chatter
of a transcendental kind.
And ev'ry one will say,
As you walk your mystic way,
"If this young man expresses himself in terms too deep for me,
Why, what a very singularly deep young man
this deep young man must be!"
Be eloquent in praise of the very dull old days

which have long since passed away,
And convince 'em, if you can, that the reign of good Queen Anne
was Culture's palmiest day.
Of course you will pooh-pooh whatever's fresh and new,
and declare it's crude and mean,
For Art stopped short in the cultivated court
of the Empress Josephine.
And ev'ryone will say,
As you walk your mystic way,
"If that's not good enough for him which is good enough for me,
Why, what a very cultivated kind of youth
this kind of youth must be!"
Any subject controversial, economic or commercial,
you must, treat with lifted brow,
Let the hoi polloi get bilious, keep the manner supercilious
of a slightly sacred cow.
If with courage Carthaginian you just offer no opinion,
you'll be hailed as a man of sense;
Endeavor to be clever and commit yourself forever
to a firm stand on defense.
And everyone will say
as you go your silent way,
"Since this young man doesn't open his mouth,
and nothing wrong says he,
Why, what a most infallibly right young man
this right young man must be!"

—W. S. Gilbert (1881)

Gilbert and Sullivan
Iolanthe **(1882), 398 performances**
7. "When You're Lying Awake (with a Dismal Headache)"

IN PERFORMANCE: ANDREW SHORE
https://www.youtube.com/watch?v=64lewe9DdQg
YouTube Key Words:
Nightmare Song English National

FULL LYRICS:

[Recitative]
Love, unrequited, robs me of my rest:
Love, hopeless love, my ardent soul encumbers:
Love, nightmare-like, lies heavy on my chest
And weaves itself into my midnight slumbers!

[Song]
When you're lying awake
With a dismal headache
And repose is taboo'd by anxiety
I conceive you may use
Any language you choose
To indulge in, without impropriety;
For your brain is on fire
The bedclothes conspire
Of usual slumber to plunder you:
First your counterpane goes
And uncovers your toes
And your sheet slips demurely from under you;
Then the blanketing tickles
You feel like mixed pickles
So terribly sharp is the pricking
And you're hot, and you're cross
And you tumble and toss
Till there's nothing 'twixt you and the ticking
Then the bedclothes all creep
To the ground in a heap
And you pick 'em all up in a tangle;
Next your pillow resigns
And politely declines
To remain at its usual angle!
Well, you get some repose
In the form of a doze
With hot eyeballs and head ever aching
But your slumbering teems
With such horrible dreams
That you'd very much better be waking;

For you dream you are crossing
The Channel, and tossing
About in a steamer from Harwich
Which is something between
A large bathing machine
And a very small second-class carriage
And you're giving a treat
(Penny ice and cold meat)
To a party of friends and relations
They're a ravenous horde
And they all came on board
At Sloane Square and South Kensington Stations
And bound on that journey
You find your attorney
(Who started that morning from Devon);
He's a bit undersized
And you don't feel surprised
When he tells you he's only eleven
Well, you're driving like mad
With this singular lad
(By the by, the ship's now a four-wheeler)
And you're playing round games
And he calls you bad names
When you tell him that "ties pay the dealer";
But this you can't stand
So you throw up your hand
And you find you're as cold as an icicle
In your shirt and your socks
(The black silk with gold clocks)
Crossing Salisbury Plain on a bicycle:
And he and the crew
Are on bicycles too
Which they've somehow or other invested in
And he's telling the tars
All the particulars
Of a company he's interested in
It's a scheme of devices
To get at low prices

All goods from cough mixtures to cables
(Which tickled the sailors)
By treating retailers
As though they were all vegetables
You get a good spadesman
To plant a small tradesman
(First take off his boots with a boot-tree)
And his legs will take root
And his fingers will shoot
And they'll blossom and bud like a fruit-tree
From the greengrocer tree
You get grapes and green pea
Cauliflower, pineapple, and cranberries
While the pastry-cook plant
Cherry brandy will grant
Apple puffs, and three corners, and Banburys
The shares are a penny
And ever so many
Are taken by Rothschild and Baring
And just as a few
Are allotted to you
You awake with a shudder despairing
You're a regular wreck
With a crick in your neck
And no wonder you snore
For your head's on the floor
And you've needles and pins
From your soles to your shins
And your flesh is a-creep
For your left leg's asleep
And you've cramp in your toes
And a fly on your nose
And some fluff in your lung
And a feverish tongue
And a thirst that's intense
And a general sense
That you haven't been sleeping in clover;
But the darkness has passed

And it's daylight at last
And the night has been long
Ditto, ditto my song
And thank goodness they're both of them over!

—W. S. Gilbert (1882)

Gilbert and Sullivan
Princess Ida **(1884), 246 performances**
8. "If You Give Me Your Attention"

IN PERFORMANCE: ARTHUR DiBIANCA
https://www.youtube.com/watch?v=K_9XH3Lyj8I
YouTube Key Words:
Give me your attention Ida 2013

[King Gama]
If you give me your attention, I will tell you what I am:
I'm a genuine philanthropist—all other kinds are sham
Each little fault of temper and each social defect
In my erring fellow creatures, I endeavor to correct
To all their little weaknesses I open people's eyes;
And little plans to snub the self-sufficient I devise;
I love my fellow creatures—I do all the good I can—
Yet everybody says I'm such a disagreeable man!
And I can't think why!
To compliments inflated I've a withering reply;
And vanity I always do my best to mortify;
A charitable action I can skillfully dissect;
And interested motives I'm delighted to detect;
I know everybody's income and what everybody earns;
And I carefully compare it with the income-tax returns;
But to benefit humanity however much I plan
Yet everybody says I'm such a disagreeable man!
And I can't think why!
I'm sure I'm no ascetic; I'm as pleasant as can be;
You'll always find me ready with a crushing repartee

I've an irritating chuckle, I've a celebrated sneer

I've an entertaining snigger, I've a fascinating leer

To everybody's prejudice I know a thing or two;

I can tell a woman's age in half a minute—and I do

But although I try to make myself as pleasant as I can

Yet everybody says I'm such a disagreeable man!

And I can't think why!

I/he can't think why!

Gilbert and Sullivan
The Mikado (1885), 672 performances
9. "I've Got a Little List"

Note: This song is sung by Ko-Ko, Lord High Executioner, in Gilbert and Sullivan's send-up of the imperial court of the Japanese emperor, or the mikado. The executioner's "little list" is all the people Ko-Ko dislikes and plans to decapitate. The original Gilbert lyrics (first performance March 14, 1885) are not only dated but also racist (e.g., they use the N-word) and are considered sexist. Virtually all modern productions use updated versions with delicious new lyrics. The version below was written and performed by Richard Suart, whose modern lyrics appear in subtitles.

IN PERFORMANCE: RICHARD SUART
(English National Opera—includes full lyrics)
https://www.youtube.com/watch?v=CWo_3CIcTBQ&t=2s
YouTube Key Words:
little list English national opera

IN PERFORMANCE: MITCHELL BUTEL
(Opera Australia)
https://www.youtube.com/watch?v=1NLV24qTnlg
YouTube Key Words:
I've Got a Little List Australia

FULL LYRICS (Gilbert original):
[Ko-Ko]

As someday it may happen that a victim must be found

I've got a little list—I've got a little list

Of society offenders who might well be underground
And who never would be missed—who never would be missed!
There's the pestilential nuisances who write for autographs—
All people who have flabby hands and irritating laughs—
All children who are up in dates, and floor you with 'em flat—
All persons who in shaking hands, shake hands with you like that—
And all third persons who on spoiling tête-á-têtes insist—
They'd none of 'em be missed—they'd none of 'em be missed!

[Chorus]
He's got 'em on the list—he's got 'em on the list;
And they'll none of 'em be missed—they'll none of 'em be missed

[Ko-Ko]
There's the banjo serenader, and the others of his race
And the piano-organist—I've got him on the list!
And the people who eat peppermint and puff it in your face
They never would be missed—they never would be missed!
Then the idiot who praises, with enthusiastic tone
All centuries but this, and every country but his own;
And the lady from the provinces, who dresses like a guy
And who "doesn't think she dances, but would rather like to try";
And that singular anomaly, the lady novelist—
I don't think she'd be missed—I'm sure she'd not he missed!

[Chorus]
He's got her on the list—he's got her on the list;
And I don't think she'll be missed—I'm sure she'll not be missed!

[Ko-Ko]
And that Nisi Prius nuisance, who just now is rather rife
The Judicial humorist—I've got him on the list!
All funny fellows, comic men, and clowns of private life—
They'd none of 'em be missed—they'd none of 'em be missed
And apologetic statesmen of a compromising kind
Such as—What d'ye call him—Thing'em-bob, and likewise—Never-mind
And St—st—st—and What's-his-name, and also You-know-who—
The task of filling up the blanks I'd rather leave to you
But it really doesn't matter whom you put upon the list
For they'd none of 'em be missed—they'd none of 'em be missed!

[Chorus]
You may put 'em on the list—you may put 'em on the list;
And they'll none of 'em be missed—they'll none of 'em be missed!

Gilbert and Sullivan
Ruddigore (1887), 288 performances
10. "My Boy, You May Take It from Me"

IN PERFORMANCE: ALED WALKER
https://www.youtube.com/watch?v=dU7416apaU4
YouTube Key Words:
My boy you may take it Minack

FULL LYRICS:
[Robin]
My boy, you may take it from me,
That of all the afflictions accurst
With which a man's saddled
And hampered and addled,
A diffident nature's the worst.
Though clever as clever can be—
A Crichton of early romance—
You must stir it and stump it,
And blow your own trumpet,
Or, trust me, you haven't a chance!
If you wish in the world to advance,
Your merits you're bound to enhance,
You must stir it and stump it,
And blow your own trumpet,
Or, trust me, you haven't a chance!

[Robin and Richard]
If you wish in the world to advance,
Your merits you're bound to enhance,
You must stir it and stump it,
And blow your own trumpet,
Or, trust me, you haven't a chance!

[Robin]

Now take, for example, my case:
I've a bright intellectual brain—
In all London city there's no one so witty—
I've thought so again and again.
I've a highly intelligent face—
My features cannot be denied—
But, whatever I try, sir, I fail in—and why, sir?
I'm modesty personified!
If you wish in the world to advance,
Your merits you're bound to enhance,
You must stir it and stump it,
And blow your own trumpet,
Or, trust me, you haven't a chance!

[Robin and Richard]

If you wish in the world to advance,
Your merits you're bound to enhance,
You must stir it and stump it,
And blow your own trumpet,
Or, trust me, you haven't a chance!

[Robin]

As a poet, I'm tender and quaint—
I've passion and fervour and grace—
From Ovid and Horace to Swinburne and Morris,
They all of them take a back place.
Then I sing and I play and I paint:
Though none are accomplished as I,
To say so were treason:
You ask me the reason?
I'm diffident, modest, and shy!
If you wish in the world to advance,
Your merits you're bound to enhance,
You must stir it and stump it,
And blow your own trumpet,
Or, trust me, you haven't a chance!

[Robin and Richard]
If you wish in the world to advance,
Your merits you're bound to enhance,
You must stir it and stump it,
And blow your own trumpet,
Or, trust me, you haven't a chance!

Gilbert and Sullivan
The Yeomen of the Guard (1888), 423 performances
11. "Oh! A Private Buffoon Is a Light-Hearted Loon"

IN PERFORMANCE: MARK STONE
https://www.youtube.com/watch?v=6ZjE7_ZS4Qk
YouTube Key Words:
A private buffoon proms

FULL LYRICS:
[Point]
Oh! a private buffoon is a light-hearted loon,
If you listen to popular rumour;
From the morn to the night he's so joyous and bright,
And he bubbles with wit and good humour!
He's so quaint and so terse,
Both in prose and in verse;
Yet though people forgive his transgression,
There are one or two rules that all family fools
Must observe, if they love their profession.
There are one or two rules,
Half-a-dozen, maybe,
That all family fools,
Of whatever degree,
Must observe if they love their profession.
If you wish to succeed as a jester, you'll need
To consider each person's auricular:
What is all right for B would quite scandalize C
(For C is so very particular);

And D may be dull, and E's very thick skull
Is as empty of brains as a ladle;
While F is F sharp, and will cry with a carp,
That he's known your best joke from his cradle!
When your humour they flout,
You can't let yourself go;
And it does put you out
When a person says, "Oh!
I have known that old joke from my cradle!"
If your master is surly, from getting up early
(And tempers are short in the morning),
An inopportune joke is enough to provoke
Him to give you, at once, a month's warning.
Then if you refrain, he is at you again,
For he likes to get value for money:
He'll ask then and there, with an insolent stare,
"If you know that you're paid to be funny?"
It adds to the tasks
Of a merry-man's place,
When your principal asks,
With a scowl on his face,
If you know that you're paid to be funny?
Comes a Bishop, maybe, or a solemn D. D.—
Oh, beware of his anger provoking!
Better not pull his hair—
Don't stick pins in his chair;
He don't understand practical joking.
If the jests that you crack have an orthodox smack,
You may get a bland smile from these sages;
But should they, by chance, be imported from France,
Half-a-crown is stopped out of your wages!
It's a general rule,
Though your zeal it may quench,
If the Family Fool
Tells a joke that's too French,
Half-a-crown is stopped out of his wages!
Though your head it may rack with a bilious attack,
And your senses with toothache you're losing,

Don't be mopy and flat—they don't fine you for that
If you're properly quaint and amusing!
Though your wife ran away with a soldier that day,
And took with her your trifle of money;
Bless your heart, they don't mind—
They're exceedingly kind—
They don't blame you—as long as you're funny!
It's a comfort to feel
If your partner should flit,
Though you suffer a deal,
They don't mind it a bit—
They don't blame you—so long as you're funny!

Gilbert and Sullivan
The Gondoliers (1889), 554 performances
12. "There Lived a King"

IN PERFORMANCE: ARTHUR DiBIANCA
https://www.youtube.com/watch?v=ie4OwwmFj8o
YouTube Key Words:
Lived a king Dibianca

FULL LYRICS:
[Don Alhambra]
There lived a King, as I've been told,
In the wonder-working days of old,
When hearts were twice as good as gold,
And twenty times as mellow.
Good-temper triumphed in his face,
And in his heart he found a place
For all the erring human race
And every wretched fellow.
When he had Rhenish wine to drink
It made him very sad to think
That some, at junket or at jink,
Must be content with toddy.

[Marcos and Giuseppe]

With toddy, must be content with toddy.

[Don Alhambra]

He wished all men as rich as he
(And he was rich as rich could be),
So to the top of every tree
Promoted everybody.

[Marcos and Giuseppe]

Now, that's the kind of King for me.
He wished all men as rich as he,
So to the top of every tree
Promoted everybody!

[Don Alhambra]

Lord Chancellors were cheap as sprats,
And Bishops in their shovel hats
Were plentiful as tabby cats—
In point of fact, too many.
Ambassadors cropped up like hay,
Prime Ministers and such as they
Grew like asparagus in May,
And Dukes were three a penny.
On every side Field-Marshals gleamed,
Small beer were Lords-Lieutenant deemed,
With Admirals the ocean teemed
All round his wide dominions.

[Marcos and Giuseppe]

All round his wide dominions.

[Don Alhambra]

And Party Leaders you might meet
In twos and threes in every street
Maintaining, with no little heat,
Their various opinions.

[Marcos and Giuseppe]

Now that's a sight you couldn't beat—

Two Party Leaders in each street
Maintaining, with no little heat,
Their various opinions.

[Don Alhambra]
That King, although no one denies
His heart was of abnormal size,
Yet he'd have acted otherwise
If he had been acuter.
The end is easily foretold,
When every blessed thing you hold
Is made of silver, or of gold,
You long for simple pewter.
When you have nothing else to wear
But cloth of gold and satins rare,
For cloth of gold you cease to care—
Up goes the price of shoddy.

[Marcos and Giuseppe]
Up goes the price of shoddy.

[Don Alhambra]
In short, whoever you may be,
To this conclusion you'll agree,
When every one is somebodee,
Then no one's anybody.

[Marcos and Giuseppe]
Now that's as plain as plain can be,
To this conclusion we agree—

[All]
When every one is somebodee,
Then no one's anybody.

—W. S. Gilbert (1889)

Gilbert and Sullivan
The Gondoliers (1889), 554 performances
13. "The Duke of Plaza-Toro"

IN PERFORMANCE: LONNIE POWELL
https://www.youtube.com/watch?v=yGFzlW7o54E
Google and YouTube Key Words:
Lonnie Powell Duke of Plaza-Toro

FULL LYRICS:
[Duke]
In enterprise of martial kind,
When there was any fighting,
He led his regiment from behind—
He found it less exciting.
But when away his regiment ran,
His place was at the fore, O—
That celebrated,
Cultivated,
Underrated
Nobleman,
The Duke of Plaza-Toro!

[All]
In the first and foremost flight, ha, ha!
You always found that knight, ha, ha!
That celebrated,
Cultivated,
Underrated
Nobleman,
The Duke of Plaza-Toro!

[Duke]
When, to evade Destruction's hand,
To hide they all proceeded,
No soldier in that gallant band
Hid half as well as he did.
He lay concealed throughout the war,
And so preserved his gore, O!

That unaffected,
Undetected,
Well-connected
Warrior,
The Duke of Plaza-Toro!

[All]
In every doughty deed, ha, ha!
He always took the lead, ha, ha!
That unaffected,
Undetected,
Well-connected
Warrior,
The Duke of Plaza-Toro!

[Duke]
When told that they would all be shot
Unless they left the service,
That hero hesitated not,
So marvelous his nerve is.
He sent his resignation in,
The first of all his corps, O!
That very knowing,
Overflowing,
Easy-going
Paladin,
The Duke of Plaza-Toro!

[All]
To men of grosser clay, ha, ha!
He always showed the way, ha, ha!
That very knowing,
Overflowing,
Easy-going
Paladin,
The Duke of Plaza-Toro!

Gilbert and Sullivan
The Gondoliers (1889), 554 performances
14. "Rising Early in the Morning"

IN PERFORMANCE: DENNIS ARROWSMITH
https://www.youtube.com/watch?v=YbM-DhoCWvU
YouTube Key Words:
2005 The Gondoliers Rising

FULL LYRICS:
[Giuseppe]
Rising early in the morning,
We proceed to light the fire,
Then our Majesty adorning
In its workaday attire,
We embark without delay
On the duties of the day.
First, we polish off some batches
Of political dispatches,
And foreign politicians circumvent;
Then, if business isn't heavy,
We may hold a Royal levee,
Or ratify some Acts of Parliament.
Then we probably review the household troops—
With the usual "Shalloo humps!" and "Shalloo hoops!"
Or receive with ceremonial and state
An interesting Eastern potentate.
After that we generally
Go and dress our private valet—
(It's a rather nervous duty—he's a touchy little man)—
Write some letters literary
For our private secretary—
He is shaky in his spelling, so we help him if we can.
Then, in view of cravings inner,
We go down and order dinner;
Then we polish the Regalia and the Coronation Plate—
Spend an hour in titivating
All our Gentlemen-in-Waiting;
Or we run on little errands for the Ministers of State.

Oh, philosophers may sing
Of the troubles of a King;
Yet the duties are delightful, and the privileges great;
But the privilege and pleasure
That we treasure beyond measure
Is to run on little errands for the Ministers of State.

[Giuseppe]
After luncheon (making merry
On a bun and glass of sherry),
If we've nothing in particular to do,
We may make a Proclamation,
Or receive a deputation—
Then we possibly create a Peer or two.
Then we help a fellow-creature on his path
With the Garter or the Thistle or the Bath,
Or we dress and toddle off in semi-state
To a festival, a function, or a fete.
Then we go and stand as sentry
At the Palace (private entry),
Marching hither, marching thither, up and down and to and fro,
While the warrior on duty
Goes in search of beer and beauty
(And it generally happens that he hasn't far to go).
He relieves us, if he's able,
Just in time to lay the table,
Then we dine and serve the coffee, and at half-past twelve or one,
With a pleasure that's emphatic,
We retire to our attic
With the gratifying feeling that our duty has been done!
Oh, philosophers may sing
Of the troubles of a King,
But of pleasures there are many and of worries there are none;
And the culminating pleasure
That we treasure beyond measure
Is the gratifying feeling that our duty has been done!

[Chorus]
Oh, philosophers may sing

Of the troubles of a King,
But of pleasures there are many and of worries there are none;
And the culminating pleasure
That we treasure beyond measure
Is the gratifying feeling that our duty has been done!

Rose Amy Fyleman (1877–1957)
Liza Lehmann (1862–1918)
15. "There Are Fairies at the Bottom of Our Garden" (1917)

IN PERFORMANCE: MICHAEL ASPINAL
https://www.youtube.com/watch?v=0riW6dUkYM4
Google and YouTube Key Words:
There are fairies in the bottom of our garden Aspinall

IN PERFORMANCE: BEA LILLIE
https://www.youtube.com/watch?v=wVo3dphCtJE
YouTube Key Words:
Fairies in the bottom of our garden Bea Lillie

FULL LYRICS:
There are fairies at the bottom of our garden!
It's not so very, very far away;
You pass the gardener's shed
and you just keep straight ahead
I do so hope they've come to stay.
There's a little wood with moss in it and beetles,
And a little stream that quietly runs through;
You wouldn't think they'd dare
to come merrymaking there,
Well, they do!
There are fairies at the bottom of our garden!
They often have a dance on summer nights;
The butterflies and bees
Make a lovely little breeze,
And the rabbits stand about and hold the lights.

Did you know that they could sit upon the moonbeams
And pick a little star to make a fan,
And dance away up there
In the middle of the air
Well, they can!
There are fairies at the bottom of our garden!
You cannot think how beautiful they are;
They all stand up and sing
When the fairy queen and king
Come gently floating down upon their car.
The king is very proud and handsome;
The queen, now can you guess who that would be?
She's a little girl all day
But at night she steals away.
Well, it's me!

—Rose Amy Fyleman (1917)

David Worton (1872–1940)
George Arthurs, Jerome Kern
16. "I Want to Sing in Opera" (1910)

IN PERFORMANCE: DAME PATRICIA ROUTLEDGE (b. 1929)
https://www.youtube.com/watch?v=ReSlfsw5iJY
YouTube Key Words:
Patricia Routledge sings 'I want to sing in Opera'

FULL LYRICS:
I'm getting so tired of these comedy songs
I want to sing something divine
I' sure and I'm certain to shine
As a star in the opera line
I simply love Wagner, Mozart, Puccini
Their music is really tip-top
So I mean to change my name Bloggs to Bloggini
And see if I can't get a "shop."

Chorus: *I want to sing in Opera*
I've got that kind of voice
I'd always sing in Opera
If I could have my choice
Signor Caruso
Told me I ought to do so
That's why I want to sing in op'ra
Sing in op-pop-pop-popera Hurrah.

I want to play Carmen I just love the part
The music's so awfully sweet
And all prima donnas I beat
If in Faust I played fair Marguerite
I'd warble and trill like a human canary
In recitative or duet
But managers seem to be just a bit wary
My chances hasn't happened as yet.

—David Worton (1910)

Part 4

SEVENTY-ONE MODERN PATTER SONGS (1920S TO THE PRESENT DAY)

ABOUT HARRY "PARKYARKARKUS" EINSTEIN

Harry Einstein (1904–58)

An American comedian, writer, and character actor specializing in Greek dialect comedy who appeared in eleven films, Einstein dropped dead in 1958 of a massive heart attack, having just performed at a Friars roast in honor of Lucille Ball and Desi Arnaz.

Lew Pollack (1895–1946)
Charles Newman (1901–78)
17. "You Can't Brush Off a Russian"

IN PERFORMANCE: HARRY "PARKYARKARKUS" EINSTEIN
www.youtube.com/watch?v=fAKNFIMT24w
YouTube Key Words:
Parkyarkarkus Brush off a Russian

I could not find this song's lyrics on the internet. They are presumably under copyright, so I can't print them here.

ABOUT NOËL COWARD

Noël Coward (1899–1973)

Coward was a showbiz legend—a delightful, debonair and suave English polymath playwright, short story writer, novelist, autobiographer, composer, lyricist, patter songster, actor, nightclub performer, clotheshorse, dandy, wit, all-around bon vivant, and world traveler.

At age eleven, Coward made his professional stage debut and went on to publish fifty plays and a dozen theatrical musicals and wrote the music and lyrics for 425 songs. His 218 film and TV credits include producing five movies, directing four others, and appearing in nineteen films. He was a favorite of the British royal family and, in particular, a longtime buddy of the Queen Mother.

A Personal Reminiscence about Las Vegas

In the summer of 1949, my parents decided to divorce. In those years that meant my father had to spend six weeks in Las Vegas to establish residency. I went along to keep him company. As I recall, there were five hotels on the strip that year. Rooms, food, and drinks cost virtually nothing; they were the bait to get gamblers to part with big bucks at blackjack, craps, roulette, and of course, the slots (a.k.a. one-armed bandits).

At age fourteen, I was not allowed inside the casinos. But the noises from within were seductive—the clink and clank of coins in the slot machines and people yelling at the crap tables: "Baby wants a new pair of shoes!" "Come on, Little Joe!" and "Eighter from Decatur!"

At the blackjack tables, the coins of the realm were today's collector's items: nineteenth-century silver dollars (mostly Morgans). A one-dollar bet in 1949 was the equivalent of eleven dollars in 2021. This was big business!

In order to draw more gamblers, the hotels would pay world-class musicians, singers, dancers, comedians, and magicians to entertain the patrons in the lounge areas. These shows were free, and drinks were on the house.

I remember three evenings: I heard Ella Fitzgerald singing scat one night and Burl Ives doing his repertoire of folk songs on another, both at the Thunderbird. Especially etched in my memory is sitting five feet away from Lena Horne while she performed her sensational rendition of "Stormy Weather."

Coward Cashes in Big in Vegas

Over the years Coward made tons of money. His net worth at his death in 1973 was estimated to be £50 million (the equivalent of US$535 million in 2021). However, in 1955 business was slow for Coward.

To the astonishment of British and American show business cognoscenti, Coward signed a contract for a month at Wilbur Clark's tacky Desert Inn for $30,000 a week ($269,000 in 2021). The incongruous promotional photo showed Coward in black tie standing alone in the desert at noon, nursing a cup of coffee. This was the 33 1/3 rpm album cover. It turned out that Coward, at age fifty-six, was in his absolute prime. Many of the patter songs that follow were photographed at that Desert Inn gig.

The question: would he draw gamblers?

Yeah, he was a smash. The publicity secured his fame in America.

In this anthology, many of Coward's videos are from that Las Vegas stint. Noël Coward was irresistible—a master entertainer and a hoot!

Noël Coward
18. "Mad Dogs and Englishmen"

IN PERFORMANCE: NOËL COWARD
https://www.youtube.com/watch?v=KkEd3WgR8qw
YouTube Key Words:
Coward Mad Dogs 1955

FULL LYRICS:
Google Key Words: mad dogs and Englishmen lyrics

Noël Coward
19. "I Went to a Marvelous Party"

IN PERFORMANCE: DAME PATRICIA ROUTLEDGE
https://www.youtube.com/watch?v=D4-comi6A3Q
YouTube Key Words:
Routledge Marvelous Party

IN PERFORMANCE: NOËL COWARD
https://www.youtube.com/watch?v=HSQ3L51UAnA
YouTube Key Words:
Marvelous Party New York

FULL LYRICS:

https://genius.com/Noel-coward-i-went-to-a-marvelous-party-lyrics

Google Key Words:

marvelous party Coward lyrics

Noël Coward

20. "Poor Uncle Harry"

IN PERFORMANCE: NOËL COWARD

https://www.youtube.com/watch?v=UFwwKbsy9Yo&list=RDQkJSOBmhdGM&index=6

YouTube Key Words:

Coward Uncle Harry 1955

FULL LYRICS:

https://genius.com/Noel-coward-uncle-harry-lyrics

Google Key Words: uncle harry lyrics

Noël Coward

21. "What's Going to Happen to the Tots?"

IN PERFORMANCE: NOËL COWARD

https://www.youtube.com/watch?v=XkIoMsdrj9s

YouTube Key Words:

Happen to the Tots 1955

FULL LYRICS:

https://genius.com/Noel-coward-whats-going-to-happen-to-the-tots-lyrics

Google Key Words:

happen to the tots lyrics

Noël Coward
22. "Why Do the Wrong People Travel?"

IN PERFORMANCE: STEFAN BEDNARCZYK
https://www.youtube.com/watch?v=7WciaaK-Aas
YouTube Key Words:
wrong people travel Bednarczyk

IN PERFORMANCE: ELAINE STRITCH
https://www.youtube.com/watch?v=81F-1o70YoM
YouTube Key Words:
Elaine Stritch why do the wrong people travel

IN PERFORMANCE: NOËL COWARD
YouTube Key Words:
Why do the wrong people Coward Matz

FULL LYRICS:
https://genius.com/Noel-coward-why-do-the-wrong-people-travel-annotated
Google Key Words:
Wrong People Travel? Lyrics

Noël Coward
23. "Why Must the Show Go On?"

IN PERFORMANCE: NOËL COWARD
https://www.youtube.com/watch?v=FxQF0AK9RjY
YouTube Key Words:
Coward show go on

FULL LYRICS:
https://tinyurl.com/y3ehw7vx
Google Key Words:
Coward show go on lyrics

Noël Coward
24. "The Stately Homes of England"

IN PERFORMANCE: NOËL COWARD
https://www.youtube.com/watch?v=8PU2ZDDGzY4
YouTube Key Words:
Stately Homes Coward

FULL LYRICS:
http://www.songlyrics.com/noel-coward/the-stately-homes-of-england-lyrics/
Google Key Words:
Stately Homes Coward Lyrics

Noël Coward
25. "Alice Is at It Again"

IN PERFORMANCE: NOËL COWARD
https://www.youtube.com/watch?v=H5-vIczW9Pk
YouTube Key Words:
Alice is at it again Coward Stott

FULL LYRICS:
https://genius.com/Noel-coward-alice-is-at-it-again-lyrics
Google Key Words:
Alice is at it again Coward lyrics

Noël Coward
26. "Don't Put Your Daughter on the Stage, Mrs. Worthington"

IN PERFORMANCE: JULIE ANDREWS
https://www.youtube.com/watch?v=rnQCI7B9GH4
YouTube Key Words:
Julie Andrews Mrs. Worthington

IN PERFORMANCE: NOËL COWARD

https://www.youtube.com/watch?v=QkJSOBmhdGM

YouTube Key Words:

best of Noel Coward, five numbers

FULL LYRICS:

https://genius.com/Noel-coward-mrs-worthington-lyrics

Google Key Words:

Don't put your daughter lyrics

Noël Coward

27. "Nina from Argentina"

IN PERFORMANCE: NOËL COWARD

https://www.youtube.com/watch?v=cnD8_2jaqA4

YouTube Key Words:

Noel Coward Nina (1955)

FULL LYRICS:

https://genius.com/Noel-coward-nina-lyrics

Google Key Words:

Nina Coward Lyrics

ABOUT COLE PORTER

Cole Porter (1891–1964)

Cole Porter was rich, brilliant, and mega-talented. He was born in Peru, Indiana, to Kate Cole, who was the daughter of James Omar "J. O." Cole. J. O. Cole was a coal and timber tycoon and, incidentally, the richest man in Indiana. While attending Yale University, Cole Porter wrote three hundred songs, including "Bulldog, bulldog, bow, wow, wow, Eli Yale!"—the famous fight song still played after touchdowns at Yale football games.

Porter's lifetime musical output was staggering. While at Yale he wrote five college shows followed by a career of forty-one additional shows (with myriad productions across the country and in London), plus the music for a ballet. His life's output: a staggering total of 841 songs, many of them classics that still generate huge royalties (e.g., "Begin the Beguine," "Night and Day," "Anything Goes") and hundreds of which made it into the top forty charts.

Porter's Near-Death Accident

In October 1937, Cole was horseback riding when his 1,000-pound mount shied, threw his rider, and then rolled on top of him, causing Porter to suffer compound fractures to his thighbones and pelvis. The ultimate injury was uncurable osteomyelitis, a calamitous bacterial infection of the bone that grew worse and worse over the next two decades.

Cole Porter underwent a series of twenty-seven ghastly operations. He spent the rest of his life dependent on wheelchairs and cane-crutches. He lived with perpetual discomfort and often excruciating pain. Yet through it all, he kept up his crazed social life and travel and creative schedules.

In 1946 Porter had an idea for a musical based on Shakespeare's rowdy comedy *The Taming of the Shrew*. It took two years of lobbying and fundraising to convince his backers that he was not damaged goods and that the idea was sound. Finally, his masterpiece—*Kiss Me, Kate*—opened December 30, 1948, and ran for 1,077 performances. It opened in London in 1951 for another 400 performances. It included two of Porter's wittiest songs, which are included in this anthology—"Where Is the Life That Late I Led" and "Brush Up Your Shakespeare."

My Favorite Porter Patter Songfest

And still Cole was far from finished. He powered on. On December 21, 1950, Porter's raciest, raunchiest musical, *Out of This World,* opened in New York. Based on the ancient Greek play *Amphitryon* by Plautus, it's the story of the randy goings-on of Greek gods on Mount Olympus. The first line of the prologue's opening song is "I Jupiter, I Rex, I Jupiter am positively teeming with sex!"

My father took me to that production at the Century Theater in New York. I know *Kiss Me, Kate* is very likely the greatest musical ever written. But God, I loved *Out of This World* (and love it still)!

Porter's rhymes are dazzling and wonderfully naughty. Example:

"I crave a pretty mortal with merry air,

And a not too plump, bump-de-bump derriere."

The Sheer Hell of Censorship

Today, this is tame stuff. But during the last three years of Prohibition, the US federal government and the states got the idea that their citizens were being corrupted by dirty movies, books, plays, and nightclub acts.

- **Example:** In 1930, under threat of government censorship, the film industry developed a production code under the aegis of lawyer Will H. Hays. The Hays office dictated what was and was not acceptable in motion pictures and in the personal conduct of actors. Thousands of screenplays and films were critiqued and forced to make changes before they could be released. Double beds were forbidden as furniture onscreen—even in the bedroom of a married couple.
- **Example:** Before Norman Mailer could publish his seminal 1948 World War II novel *The Naked and the Dead*, he was forced to flyspeck the manuscript and change a much-used four-letter word to a nonexistent three-letter word—"fug."

When outspoken stage and screen actress Tallulah Bankhead was introduced to Mailer at a party, she reportedly said, "Oh yes, you're the young man who doesn't know how to spell 'fuck.'"

- **Example:** Undercover detectives surreptitiously recorded comic Lenny Bruce's nightclub act on two occasions. He was summarily arrested, carted offstage, and indicted for "violating New York Penal Code 1140, barring obscene materials that could aid in the 'corruption of morals of youth and others,' and faced a maximum punishment of three years in prison." In the 1960s, Bruce was harassed and charged with obscenity myriad times across the country.
- **Example:** Broadway was no easier. The censors drove Porter and his producers nuts with their demands to clean up *Out of This World*. Here's part of the letter received during the Boston tryouts:

CITY OF BOSTON
OFFICE OF THE MAYOR
CITY HALL
LICENSING DIVISION
John B. Hines, Mayor
Walter K. Milliken, Chief

November 29, 1950

Mr. Michael Kavanaugh
Schubert Theatre

Boston

Dear Mr. Kavanaugh:
   We would appreciate the following eliminations being made in "Out of This World" at the Schubert Theatre.

All irreverent use of "God."

Act 1 "They Couldn't Compare to You" Suggest a substitution for the line that sounded like "saving my urgings for several Vestal Virgins" Mercury at completion of song to modify action with hands on girls leg.

Ballet at end of Act 1 to be greatly modified.

Act 2 Scene 1 Juno "old bag"

Helen "sexual insecurity"

Niki scene 3 Blessing himself after shooting Juno.

Scene 8 "Nobody's Chasing Me": cut "goosing me"

Thanking you for your past cooperation, I am

Very truly yours

Beatrice J. Whelton

The demand that most irritated me was the forced change of Cole Porter's best patter song in the show, "They Couldn't Compare to You."

https://www.youtube.com/watch?v=98HEiL0Uin0
YouTube Key Words:
Abud They Couldn't Compare

   This number is sung by the messenger of the gods, Mercury, who boasts of having affairs with famous women throughout history, fiction, and mythology. Here's the final stanza:

When betwixt Nell Gwyn and Anne Boleyn
I was forced to make my choice

I became so confused I was even amused
And abused by Peggy Joyce.
There was Melisande, a platinum blonde,
How I loved to ruffle her locks.
There was bright Aurora and then Pandora
Who let me open her …

The censors would not allow the line "open her box" to rhyme with "locks"—"box" being occasional slang for "vagina." So the chorus jumped in with "They couldn't compare to you …"

Another Porter Song That Would Corrupt the Viewers' Morals

Check out "Nobody's Chasing Me," sung by Juno (Charlotte Greenwood), the cuckolded wife of Jupiter:

Ravel is chasing Debussy
The aphid chases the pea
The gander's chasing the goosey
But nobody's goosing me.
Nobody!
Nobody's chasing me.

You can see in the Boston censorship letter that Porter was told to eliminate "Nobody's goosing me." In 1955 I met William Redfield, who played Mercury, and we talked about the censorship problem. He shook his head and referenced this song and the following verse:

The cook is chasing the chicken
The peewee some we peewee
The cat is taking a lickin'
But nobody's taking me.

You betcha the censors would not allow the last line to be "But nobody's lickin' me." All of this was in flat violation of the First Amendment:

Congress shall make no law respecting an establishment of religion, or prohibiting the free exercise thereof; or abridging the freedom of speech, or of the press.

The idea that these slightly naughty lyrics would possibly aid in the "corruption of morals of youth and others" is preposterous.

You gotta love Cole Porter for making those bluenose prudes earn their pay.

Porter Biopics

Two films were made about Cole Porter's life and work:

- ***Night and Day* (1946)**

Cary Grant, Alexis Smith, Monty Wooley (playing himself), Ginny Simms, Jane Wyman

Night and Day is an okay, workman-like film, well written, elegantly photographed, and directed by one of Hollywood's greatest (and most prolific, with 181 films) directors, Michael Curtiz (*Casablanca, Yankee Doodle Dandy*). The film was released eighteen years before Porter's death and has a feel-good happy ending, which turned out not to be the case in real life.

- ***De-Lovely* (2004)**

Kevin Kline, Ashley Judd, Jonathan Pryce

In my opinion, this is a kaleidoscopic masterpiece. Directed by Irwin Winkler, the film captures Porter's genius, curious marriage, dazzling career, and tragic end.

Cole Porter

28. "Let's Do It"

IN PERFORMANCE: Cole Porter

https://www.youtube.com/watch?v=7qf_QorYgDE

YouTube Key Words:

Let's Fall in Love Cole Porter

FULL LYRICS:

https://genius.com/Cole-porter-lets-do-it-lets-fall-in-love-lyrics

Google Key Words

Let's Do it lyrics genius

Noël Coward
29. "Let's Do It" (Coward's Racy Rewrite of Cole Porter)

IN PERFORMANCE: NOËL COWARD
https://www.youtube.com/watch?v=Ykan2f1I0pc
YouTube Key Words:
Let's Do It Noel Coward

FULL LYRICS:
https://genius.com/Noel-coward-lets-do-it-lets-fall-in-love-lyrics
Google Key Words:
Let's do it Coward lyrics

Cole Porter
Let's Face It
30. "Let's Not Talk about Love"

IN PERFORMANCE: DANNY KAYE
https://www.youtube.com/watch?v=VXqszcjzz4M
YouTube Key Words:
Danny Kaye Let's Not Talk about Love

FULL LYRICS:
https://tinyurl.com/yxvuegcy
Google Key Words:
Let's Not Talk about Love Lyrics

Cole Porter
Out of This World
31. "They Couldn't Compare to You"

IN PERFORMANCE: GEORGE ABUD
https://www.youtube.com/watch?v=98HEiL0Uin0

YouTube Key Words:

Abud They Couldn't Compare

IN PERFORMANCE: WILLIAM REDFIELD

https://www.youtube.com/watch?v=vHbFr6YYTb8

YouTube Key Words:

They couldn't compare to you Redfield

FULL LYRICS:

https://tinyurl.com/y6b3auza

Google Key Words:

They couldn't compare to you redfield

Cole Porter
Out of This World
32. "What Do You Think about Men?"

IN PERFORMANCE: GLORIA SWANSON, BARBARA EDEN, BROOKE SHIELDS

https://www.youtube.com/watch?v=8CuOmMzG_-4

YouTube Key Words:

Swanson, Shields think about men

IN PERFORMANCE: CHARLOTTE GREENWOOD, PRISCILLA GILLETTE, BARBARA ASHLEY

https://www.youtube.com/watch?v=G4kY2NgN80Y

YouTube Key Words:

Out of This World What Do You Think about Men

FULL LYRICS:

https://www.allmusicals.com/lyrics/outofthisworld/whatdoyouthinkaboutmen.htm

Google Key Words:

Out of this world what do you think about men lyrics

Cole Porter

Out of This World

33. "I Sleep Easier Now"

IN PERFORMANCE: CHARLOTTE GREENWOOD

https://www.youtube.com/watch?v=_pLLVClgeF0

YouTube Key Words:

I sleep easier now Greenwood

IN PERFORMANCE: MRS. MILLER (ELVA RUBY CONNES)

https://www.youtube.com/watch?v=OAUVD8E9sl8

YouTube Key Words:

I sleep easier now Mrs. Miller

FULL LYRICS:

https://www.allmusicals.com/lyrics/outofthisworld/isleepeasiernow.htm

Google Key Words

I sleep easier now lyrics

Cole Porter

Out of This World

34. "I Jupiter, I Rex, I'm Positively Teeming with Sex"

IN PERFORMANCE: WILLIAM REDFIELD, GEORGE JONGEYANS-GAYNES

https://www.youtube.com/watch?v=QMVu4bfojsQ

YouTube Key Words:

I Jupiter I Rex Redfield

FULL LYRICS:

https://www.allmusicals.com/lyrics/outofthisworld/ijupiterirex.htm

Google Key Words:

I Jupiter I Rex lyrics

Cole Porter
Out of This World
35. "Cherry Pies Ought to Be You"

IN PERFORMANCE: WILLIAM REDFIELD, BARBARA ASHLEY, DAVID BURNS, CHARLOTTE GREENWOOD
https://www.youtube.com/watch?v=yJRWEjU-k6c
YouTube Key Words:
Out of this world cherry pies ought

IN PERFORMANCE: FRANK SINATRA, ROSEMARY CLOONEY
https://www.youtube.com/watch?v=uDxWBdFQOcs
YouTube Key Words:
Sinatra Cherry Pies ought to be you

FULL LYRICS:
https://www.jiosaavn.com/lyrics/from-this-moment-on:-out-of-this-world:-cherry-pies-ought-to-be-you-lyrics/SCsyBQVqYAI
Google Key Words:
Moment on cherry pies lyrics

Cole Porter
Out of This World
36. "Nobody's Chasing Me"

IN PERFORMANCE: CHARLOTTE GREENWOOD
https://www.youtube.com/watch?v=ilzmpBJlnG0&list=RDilzmpBJlnG0&start_radio=1
YouTube Key Words:
Nobody's chasing Greenwood

FULL LYRICS:

https://www.allmusicals.com/lyrics/outofthisworld/nobodyschasingme.htm

Google Key Words:

Nobody's chasing me lyrics

Cole Porter

37. "You're the Top"

IN PERFORMANCE: SUTTON FOSTER, COLIN DONNELL

https://www.youtube.com/watch?v=rZViKrO-pMo

YouTube Key Words:

You're the top Sutton Foster

FULL LYRICS:

https://genius.com/Cole-porter-youre-the-top-lyrics

Google Key Words:

You're the Top Genius Lyrics

IRVING BERLIN'S (ALLEGED) REALLY BAWDY LYRICS

https://slate.com/news-and-politics/2005/06/another-porter-riddle.html

Google Key Words:

Another Porter Riddle

Cole Porter

Kiss Me, Kate

38. "Where Is the Life That Late I Led?"

IN PERFORMANCE: ALFRED DRAKE

https://www.youtube.com/watch?v=-E2GM5bB3IY&t=22s

YouTube Key Words:

Alfred Drake where is the life

FULL LYRICS:

https://tinyurl.com/yxcdtnk7

Google Key Words:

Life that late I led Porter Genius

Cole Porter

Kiss Me, Kate

39. "Brush Up Your Shakespeare"

IN PERFORMANCE: MICHAEL JIBSON AND JAMES DOHERTY

https://www.youtube.com/watch?v=ocq0-LINGyw

YouTube Key Words:

Brush up your Shakespeare Jibson

FULL LYRICS:

https://www.lyrics.com/lyric/10004796/Cole+Porter/Brush+Up+Your+Shakespeare

Google Key Words:

brush up your Shakespeare lyrics

Cole Porter

40. "Tale of the Oyster"

IN PERFORMANCE: SARA MATTOX

https://www.youtube.com/watch?v=62TKNKEnlFo

YouTube Key Words:

Tale of the Oyster Mattox

FULL LYRICS:

https://genius.com/Cole-porter-the-tale-of-the-oyster-lyrics

Google Key Words:

Tale of the Oyster lyrics

Michael Stewart (1924–87)
Cy Coleman (1929–2004)
Barnum
41. "The Museum Song"

IN PERFORMANCE: MARC GINSBERG.
https://www.youtube.com/watch?v=z90Ht1Fl7lA
YouTube Key Words:
Marc Ginsburg Museum Song

FULL LYRICS:
https://tinyurl.com/y5np87em
Google Key Words:
Museum Song Lyrics

Michael Stewart
Jerry Herman (1931-2019)
Hello, Dolly!
42. "Penny in My Pocket"

IN PERFORMANCE: DAVID HYDE PIERCE
https://www.youtube.com/watch?v=cNr4lO_v0XM
YouTube Key Words:
Penny in my pocket (Hello Dolly) Pierce

FULL LYRICS::
https://tinyurl.com/y47o4bd9
Google Key Words:
Penny in my pocket lyrics

ABOUT DANNY KAYE AND SYLVIA FINE
Danny Kaye (1911–87)
Sylvia Fine (1913–91)

Danny Kaye, the Greatest Patter Songster Ever

Always in the background—and frequently playing piano for Danny Kaye—was the brilliant, multitalented Sylvia Fine, the life partner Kaye married in 1940. Fine wrote most of Kaye's best patter songs.

On January 23, 1941, a supernova burst onto the stage of Broadway's Alvin Theater on West Fifty-Second Street. The show was *Lady in the Dark* by Moss Hart, with music by Kurt Weill and lyrics by Ira Gershwin. That brilliant exploding star was thirty-year-old Danny Kaye. He performed perhaps the most challenging, tongue-tripping patter song ever written: "Tchaikovsky and Other Russian Composers."

Thirty years later, Kaye reprised the Russian composers song in an interview with Dick Cavett, where he ripped through the names of fifty-six Russian classical composers in a brain-spinning thirty-seven seconds.

What's more, he did it with such precise diction that you can hear every name.

IN PERFORMANCE: Danny Kaye
https://www.youtube.com/watch?v=dCCaMqxi8U4
YouTube Key Words:
Kaye 56 Russians Cavett

Note: Check out number 47 for three additional versions of this Ira Gershwin classic. Larry Raben with blow your socks off.

Sylvia Fine
43. "Anatole of Paris"

IN PERFORMANCE: DANNY KAYE
https://www.youtube.com/watch?v=uJ9bnC1v1xc
YouTube Key Words:
Anatole of Paris

FULL LYRICS:
https://genius.com/Danny-kaye-anatole-of-paris-lyrics
Google Key Words:
Anatole of Paris Lyrics

Sylvia Fine and Max Liebman
44. "Up in Arms Theater Lobby Number"

IN PERFORMANCE: DANNY KAYE
https://www.youtube.com/watch?v=54r75MVXi1o
YouTube Key Words:
Theater Lobby Number (the Lobby Number)

]
FULL LYRICS:
https://www.loc.gov/resource/ihas.200183674.0/?sp=1
Google Key Words:
Image 1 Lobby Number Library of Congress

Danny Kaye
45. "Danny Kaye as the Professor of Music"

IN PERFORMANCE: DANNY KAYE
https://www.youtube.com/watch?v=DP1J4pObRIE
YouTube Key Words:
Danny Kaye as the Professor of Music.mpg

Note: The lyrics are impossible to capture. You have to see and hear it to believe it!

Adolph Green (1914–2002)
Betty Comden (1917–2006)
Roger Edens (1905–70)
46. "Tongue Twisters"

IN PERFORMANCE: DANNY KAYE
https://www.youtube.com/watch?v=B9BrR4u30I4
Google Key Words:
tongue twisters Danny Kaye

FULL LYRICS:

https://www.lyrics.com/lyric/948600/Danny+Kaye/Tongue+Twisters

Google Key Words:

Tongue Twisters Lyrics

ABOUT IRA GERSHWIN (1896–1983)

In my opinion, with "Tchaikovsky and Other Russian Composers," Ira Gershwin wrote the ultimate patter song in terms of rhyming wizardry and pushing performers to their verbal limits. Following are three versions of this splendid war horse.

• **Traditional:** Michael Feinstein in an elegant supper club rendition.

• **Original:** Danny Kaye, who introduced it in *Lady in the Dark* in 1941.

• **Rat-a-tat-tat patter song pyrotechnics**: Larry Raben, who performs this song three times—fast, faster, and at the speed of light. In the final version, he recites the fifty-six Russian composers' names in a blistering thirty-four seconds, whereupon Raben ends up on the floor.

An Aside:

Lyricist Ira Gershwin (brother of fabled composer George Gershwin) struggled to string together enough Russian composers to make the song work and slipped in the name of a non-classical Russian composer in the following line: "And Sokoloff and Kopyloff, Dukelsky, and Klenowsky."

Dukelsky's full name was Vladimir Aleksandrovich Dukelsky (1903–69). In the early 1920s, Dukelsky's pal George Gershwin suggested he Americanize his name, and Vladimir Dukelsky became Vernon Duke, composer of *Ziegfeld Follies* in 1934 (lyrics by E. Y. "Yip" Harburg) and 1936 (lyrics by Ira Gershwin) as well as *Cabin in the Sky* (lyrics by John LaTouche). Among Duke's hit popular songs were "I Can't Get Started," "Autumn in New York," and "Taking a Chance on Love."

Ira Gershwin
Kurt Weill (1900–50)
Lady in the Dark
47. "Tchaikovsky and Other Russians"

IN PERFORMANCE: MICHAEL FEINSTEIN

https://www.youtube.com/watch?v=QTjVP21XrWw

YouTube Key Words:

Michael Feinstein Tchaikovsky and other Russians

IN PERFORMANCE: DANNY KAYE, SYLVIA FINE

https://www.youtube.com/watch?v=8DEJOwLQhJQ

YouTube Key Words:

Kaye Tchaikovsky John Foia

IN PERFORMANCE: LARRY RABEN

https://www.youtube.com/watch?v=fFILIq6n-zI

YouTube Key Words:

Larry Raben Tchaikovsky

FULL LYRICS:

https://genius.com/Danny-kaye-tschaikowsky-and-other-russians-lyrics

Google Key Words: |

Danny Kaye Tchaikovsky Lyrics Genius

Meredith Willson (1902–84)

The Music Man

48. "Ya Got Trouble (Right Here in River City)"

IN PERFORMANCE: ROBERT PRESTON

CAMEO: BUDDY HACKETT

https://www.youtube.com/watch?v=LI_Oe-jtgdI

YouTube Key Words:

Music Man Ya Got Trouble

FULL LYRICS:

https://genius.com/Meredith-willson-ya-got-trouble-lyrics

Google Key Words:

Ya Got Trouble lyrics Genius Lyrics

Michael Korie (b. 1955)
Scott Frankel (b. 1963)
Grey Gardens
49. "The Revolutionary Costume" (Speaking)

IN PERFORMANCE: CHRISTINE EBERSOLE
https://www.youtube.com/watch?v=gdh8EoYoAoM
YouTube Key Words:
Grey Gardens 2007 Tony Performance

FULL LYRICS:
https://www.allmusicals.com/lyrics/greygardens/therevolutionarycostumefortoday.
htm
Google Key Words:
Revolutionary Costume for Today lyrics

Eric Idle (b. 1943)
Spamalot
50. "You Won't Succeed on Broadway"

IN PERFORMANCE: DAVID HYDE PIERCE
https://www.youtube.com/watch?v=R6VKf6bXCCo
YouTube Key Words:
Pierce You Won't Succeed on Broadway

FULL LYRICS:
https://tinyurl.com/y4b9oyda
Google Key Words:
You won't succeed on Broadway lyrics

Newman Levy (1888–1966)
Opera Guyed (1923)
51. "Tahis"

IN PERFORMANCE: WILLARD LOSINGER
https://www.youtube.com/watch?v=xh56tHJIpQo
YouTube Key Words:
Willard Losinger performing tahis

FULL LYRICS:
http://www.blueridgejournal.com/poems/nl1-thais.htm
Google Key Words:
Alexandria (Thais) Newman Levy

Rudyard Kipling (?) (1865–1936)
52. "The Bastard King of England"

IN PERFORMANCE: WILLARD LOSINGER
https://www.youtube.com/watch?v=9DLdlzgtEeU
YouTube Key Words:
Losinger Performing Bastard King of England

FULL LYRICS:
http://www.traditionalmusic.co.uk/folk-song-lyrics/Bastard_King_of_England.htm
Google Key Words:
Bastard King of England Lyrics

Frank Loesser (1910–69)
Guys and Dolls
53. "Adelaide's Lament"

IN PERFORMANCE: RIA JONES
https://www.youtube.com/watch?v=5ADNXKJRxro

FULL LYRICS:
https://genius.com/Frank-loesser-adelaides-lament-lyrics
Google Keywords:
Develop a Cold Lyrics

Frank Loesser
Guys and Dolls
54. "Marry the Man Today"

IN PERFORMANCE: VERONICA J. KUEHN, AUDREY CARDWELL
https://www.youtube.com/watch?v=AjXOO81_Cdc
YouTube Key Words:
Marry the man Kuehn

FULL LYRICS:
https://genius.com/Frank-loesser-marry-the-man-today-lyrics
Google Key Words:
Marry the man today lyrics

ABOUT TOM LEHRER

The Bizarre Intersection of a Higher Mathematician and the Lower-Brow World of Patter Songs

Tom Lehrer (b. 1928)
To me, the most fascinating and unusual inductee into what I guess is a fledgling Patter Song Hall of Fame is Thomas Andrew Lehrer, magna cum laude, Harvard University graduate in the rarified world of higher mathematics.

Mathematics? Patter songs? Huh?

I can think of just two mathematicians who changed history—and the world—in the twentieth century: Albert Einstein and Alan Turing.

Albert Einstein (1879–1955)

- Albert Einstein decided to move to the United States, where he became a member of the faculty at Princeton's Institute of Advanced Study. Here is the lede of Einstein's letter to the US president in 1939:

```
                                    Albert Einstein
                                      Old Grove Rd.
                                       Nassau Point
                          Peconic, Long Island

                               August 2nd, 1939
```

```
F.D. Roosevelt
President of the United States
White House
Washington, D.C.

Sir,

Some recent work by E. Fermi and L. Szilard, which has been
communicated to me in manuscript, leads me to expect that
the element uranium may be turned into a new and important
source of energy in the immediate future.

Certain aspects of the situation which has arisen seem to
call for watchfulness and, if necessary, quick action on
the part of the Administration. I believe therefore that it
is my duty to bring to your attention the following facts
and recommendations …
```

```
The resultant atomic bomb is acknowledged to have shortened
World War II by at least a year and a half and saved as many
as ten million lives. Atomic energy may well save the planet.
```

Alan Turing (1912–54)

- London-born Alan Turing graduated from the University of Cambridge and earned his PhD from Princeton in 1938. In 1939 he went to work at the super-secret facility at Bletchley Park outside London. His pioneering work on the Enigma machine (basically the world's first computer) cracked Nazi Germany's military and diplomatic codes. Turing's work is generally acknowledged to have shortened World War II by two years. And of course, computers changed the world.

Note: If you haven't seen *The Imitation Game* about Turing and Bletchley Park—with Benedict Cumberbatch as Alan Turing—rent it! It is riveting!

Tom Lehrer is a fascinating guy—a former child prodigy. His extraordinary self-made careers in higher mathematics, vanity recordings, and world tours and—most important—in creating risqué and often censored patter songs, filled with delicious double-entendres based on sensational headline stories of his era, are brilliantly recounted and annotated in Wikipedia. He's a wonderful one of a kind.

https://en.wikipedia.org/wiki/Tom_Lehrer
Google Key Words:
Tom Lehrer Wikipedia

Tom Lehrer
55. "The Elements"

IN PERFORMANCE: TOM LEHRER
Note: Sung to the tune of Sir Arthur Sullivan's Major-General Song
https://www.youtube.com/watch?v=AcS3NOQnsQM
YouTube Key Words:
Tom Lehrer The Elements performance Copenhagen

LEHRER'S "ELEMENTS" ANIMATED! YOU GOTTA SEE THIS!
https://www.youtube.com/watch?v=zGM-wSKFBpo
YouTube Key Words:
Tom Lehrer Elements Animated

FULL LYRICS:
https://genius.com/Tom-lehrer-the-elements-lyrics
Google Key Words:
The elements Tom Lehrer lyrics

Tom Lehrer
56. "The New Math"

IN PERFORMANCE: TOM LEHRER
https://www.youtube.com/watch?v=UIKGV2cTgqA
YouTube Key Words:
New Math Lehrer

FULL LYRICS:
https://genius.com/Tom-lehrer-new-math-lyrics
Google Key Words:
Lehrer, New Math Lyrics

Tom Lehrer
57. "Werner Von Braun (The Old Nazi)"

IN PERFORMANCE: TOM LEHRER
https://www.youtube.com/watch?v=TjDEsGZLbio&t=4s
YouTube Key Words:
Tom Lehrer Wernher von Braun

FULL LYRICS:
https://genius.com/Tom-lehrer-wernher-von-braun-lyrics
Google Key Words:
Lehrer Von Braun Lyrics

Tom Lehrer
58. MLF Lullaby

IN PERFORMANCE: TOM LEHRER
https://www.youtube.com/watch?v=3j20voPS0gI
YouTube Key Words:
MLF Lullaby Tom Lehrer

FULL LYRICS
https://genius.com/Tom-lehrer-mlf-lullaby-lyrics
Google Key Words:
MLF Lullaby Lyrics Lehrer

Tom Lehrer
59. "Who's Next?"

IN PERFORMANCE: TOM LEHRER
https://www.youtube.com/watch?v=oRLON3ddZIw
YouTube Key Words:
Tom Lehrer Who's Next

FULL LYRICS:
https://www.lyricsfreak.com/t/tom+lehrer/whos+next_10233302.html
Google Key Words:
Lehrer who's next lyricsfreak

Tom Lehrer
60. "Poisoning Pigeons in the Park"

Note: At some point the city of Boston dealt with the guano problem by feeding strychnine-laced birdseed to pigeons.

IN PERFORMANCE: TOM LEHRER
https://www.youtube.com/watch?v=yhuMLpdnOjY
YouTube Key Words:
Poisoning pigeons lehrer

FULL LYRICS:
Google Key Words:
Poisoning Pigeons in the Park lyrics

Tom Lehrer

61. "The Vatican Rag"

Note: Inspired by the notorious Second Vatican Council of 1962.

IN PERFORMANCE: TOM LEHRER
https://www.youtube.com/watch?v=pvhYqeGp_Do
YouTube Key Words:
Vatican Rag Lehrer

FULL LYRICS:
https://www.elyrics.net/read/t/tom-lehrer-lyrics/the-vatican-rag-lyrics.html
Google Key Words:
Vatican Rag Lyrics

Tom Lehrer
62. "Be Prepared"

IN PERFORMANCE: TOM LEHRER
https://www.youtube.com/watch?v=gkrheaWuShU
YouTube Key Words:
Tom Lehrer be prepared concert live

FULL LYRICS:
https://genius.com/Tom-lehrer-be-prepared-lyrics
Google Key Words:
Be prepared lyrics Lehrer genius

Tom Lehrer
63. "A Christmas Carol"

IN PERFORMANCE: TOM LEHRER
https://www.youtube.com/watch?v=DtZR3lJobjw
YouTube Key Words:
A Christmas Carol Lehrer YouTube

FULL LYRICS:

https://genius.com/Tom-lehrer-a-christmas-carol-lyrics

Google Key Words:

Christmas Carol Tom Lehrer lyrics Genius

Tom Lehrer
64. "Alma"

IN PERFORMANCE: TOM LEHRER

https://www.youtube.com/watch?v=QL6KgbrGSKQ

YouTube Key Words:

Tom Lehrer Alma concert live (1965)

FULL LYRICS:

https://genius.com/Tom-lehrer-alma-lyrics

Google Key Words:

Alma Tom Lehrer lyrics

Tom Lehrer
65. "Chanukah in Santa Monica"

IN PERFORMANCE: TOM LEHRER

https://www.youtube.com/watch?v=LslsgH3-UFU

YouTube Key Words:

Chanukah in Santa Monica analog 36

IN PERFORMANCE: GAY MEN'S CHORUS

https://www.youtube.com/watch?v=MehTnsDVvU4

YouTube Key Words:

Chanukah in Santa Monica GMCLAvideo

FULL LYRICS:

https://genius.com/Tom-lehrer-im-spending-hanukkah-in-santa-monica-lyrics

Google Key Words:

Chanukah in Santa Monica Lehrer Lyrics

Tom Lehrer
66. "Smut"

IN PERFORMANCE: TOM LEHRER
https://www.youtube.com/watch?v=iaHDBL7dVgs&t=63s
YouTube Key Words:|
Tom Lehrer Smut

FULL LYRICS
https://genius.com/Tom-lehrer-smut-lyrics
Google Key Words:|
Tom Lehrer Smut Lyrics

Tom Lehrer
67. "I Hold Your Hand in Mine"

IN PERFORMANCE: TOM LEHRER
https://www.youtube.com/watch?v=I9C2v1oLXQo&t=13s
YouTube Key Words:
I hold your hand in mine Lehrer Live Film

FULL LYRICS:
https://genius.com/Tom-lehrer-i-hold-your-hand-in-mine-lyrics
Google Key Words:
Lehrer I hold your hand in mine lyrics genius

Tom Lehrer
68. "Oedipus Rex"

IN PERFORMANCE: TOM LEHRER
https://www.youtube.com/watch?v=mScdJURKGWM
YouTube Key Words:
Tom Lehrer Oedipus Rex

FULL LYRICS:
https://www.stlyrics.com/songs/t/tomlehrer3903/oedipusrex348431.html
Google Key Words:
Oedipus Rex Lehrer lyrics

Phil Harris (1904–95)
Tex Williams (1917–85)
Merle Travis (1917–83)
69. "Smoke! Smoke! Smoke! (That Cigarette)"

IN PERFORMANCE: PHIL HARRIS
https://www.youtube.com/watch?v=87TcFNqKQbg
YouTube Key Words:
Phil Harris Smoke, Smoke Johnny Cash

FULL LYRICS:
https://genius.com/Jimmy-dean-smoke-smoke-smoke-that-cigarette-lyrics
Google Key Words:
Smoke Smoke Jimmy Dean Metro Lyrics

Rufus Thomas (1917–2001)
70. "The Preacher and the Bear"

IN PERFORMANCE: PHIL HARRIS
https://www.youtube.com/watch?v=s5V_rymAy04
YouTube Key Words:

Harris Preacher and the Bear (1961)

FULL LYRICS:

https://genius.com/Phil-harris-the-preacher-and-the-bear-lyrics

Google Key Words:

The preacher and the bear lyrics

Phil Harris
71. "Darktown Poker Club"

IN PERFORMANCE: PHIL HARRIS
https://www.youtube.com/watch?v=poGrRIuvJlY
YouTube Key Words:
Phil Harris darktown poker club 1946

FULL LYRICS:
http://www.songlyrics.com/phil-harris/the-dark-town-poker-club-lyrics/
Google Key Words:
Darktown poker club lyrics

Phil Harris
72. "He's His Own Grandpa"

IN PERFORMANCE: PHIL HARRIS
https://www.youtube.com/watch?v=LxIdLGg7rZM
YouTube Key Words:
He's his own grandpa Phil Harris

FULL LYRICS:
http://www.songlyrics.com/phil-harris/he-s-his-own-grandpa-lyrics/
Google Key Words:
He's his own grandpa lyrics

Phil Harris

73. "That's What I Like about the South"

IN PERFORMANCE: PHIL HARRIS

https://www.youtube.com/watch?v=A_dK0W0qfRo&t=3s

Google Key Words

Phil Harris that's what I like about the south

FULL LYRICS:

https://genius.com/Phil-harris-thats-what-i-like-about-the-south-lyrics

Google Key Words

Phil Harris that's what I like about the south Lyrics

Lorenz Hart (1895–1943)

Richard Rogers (1902–79)

A Connecticut Yankee

74. "To Keep My Love Alive"

IN PERFORMANCE: ELAINE STRITCH

https://www.youtube.com/watch?v=X_H9yGF36Rc

YouTube Key Words:

Keep love alive Stritch

FULL LYRICS:

https://genius.com/Rodgers-and-hart-to-keep-my-love-alive-lyrics

Google Key Words:

Keep my love alive lyrics genius

Richard Wilbur (1921–2017)
Leonard Bernstein's *Candide*
75. "Pangloss's Song"

Note: America's poet laureate, Wilbur was one of five librettists for *Candide*, along with Leonard Bernstein, Stephen Sondheim, John LaTouche, and Lillian Hellman.

IN PERFORMANCE: RICHARD WILBUR (WATCH FIRST)
https://www.youtube.com/watch?v=avq_HiibCcg
YouTube Key Words:
Wilbur reading Pangloss

IN PERFORMANCE: ADOLPH GREEN AND LEONARD BERNSTEIN
https://www.youtube.com/watch?v=YzyJMhI_WAQ
YouTube Key Words:
Candide dear boy Green

FULL LYRICS:
https://genius.com/Leonard-bernstein-dear-boy-lyrics
Google Key Words:
Dear Boy, Bernstein Genius Lyrics

ABOUT MADAME SPIVY

Bertha Levine (1906–71)
In the late 1940s a friend of my family used to frequent Spivy's Roof (1940–51), a small, intimate nightclub on the ninth floor of a nondescript building on East Fifty-Ninth Street in Manhattan. This friend of the family knew of my interest in patter songs and gave me *Seven Sophisticated Gay Songs by Spivy*, an album consisting of multiple 78 rpm records. This was racy adult stuff back in those days. I played the records constantly and knew all the words. I loved it!

The founder/owner of Spivy's Roof was Bertha Levine—pianist, composer, lyricist, and entertainer, a.k.a. Madame Spivy (pronounced "spivvy"). The club became a hangout for showbiz greats, who sometimes performed there. Among them were Judy Garland, Moms Mabley, Liberace, Bea Arthur, Mabel Mercer, and Judy Holiday. Paul Lynde shared his memories of Spivy and the club.

Paul Lynde Talks about Spivy's Roof
https://www.youtube.com/watch?v=JpnsiM3nZ3w
YouTube Key Words:
Paul Lynde talks about Spivy's Roof

Madame Spivy entertained her patrons with a delicious repertoire of patter/party songs. From her Wikipedia bio:

> In 1939, the *New York Times* wrote that "Spivy's material, witty, acid, and tragicomic, is better than most of the essays one hears about town, and her delivery is that of a sophisticated artist on her own grounds. She knows the value of surprise in punching a line, she uses understatement unerringly, and her piano accompaniment is superb."

A Unique Business Philosophy

In a supper club all is atmosphere. Without atmosphere you are a couple of chairs and tables in a bare room. You've got to make the trade feel like guests in a parlor of gaiety. The customer is more usually tight than right.

—Madame Spivy, qtd. in her obituary, *New York Times*, January 10, 1971

Madame Spivy wrote and composed much of her own material in addition to working with fledgling composers and lyricists who went on to great careers. One of her very young lyricist partners—in his twenties at the time—was John LaTouche ("Toosh" to his friends), who later wrote two major hit songs: "Taking a Chance on Love" from his Broadway musical *Cabin in the Sky* (music by Vernon Duke) and "Lazy Afternoon" from his off-Broadway *The Golden Apple* (music by Jerome Moross).

Alas, in 1956 John LaTouche dropped dead of a heart attack at age forty-one—a tragic loss for American theater.

In researching *Bawdy Jokes and Patter Songs,* I was thrilled to stumble upon three long-lost lyrics by John LaTouche as originally performed nightly by Madame Spivy. You can savor them by following the links and key words provided for LaTouche's songs in the following section.

Enjoy!

IMPORTANT NOTE: Spivy in performance is hard to find. Most of these songs are not on YouTube. Rather they are buried deep on the Internet and can be accessed via Google.

Here is the link to Madame Spivy's albums.
https://www.queermusicheritage.com/oct2000ms.html
Google Key Words:
Madame Spivy – Queer Music Heritage

Here's the Drill:
1. **When the album cover appears: Scroll Down.**
2. You will come immediately to: **1939**
3. You will find the first six song titles printed in purple or blue.
4. Each of these purple and blue titles is a link to the song. Click on the words.
5. **To access the last two songs: Scroll Down.**
6. You will come eventually to: **1947.**
7. The final two songs titles are in blue or purple. These are links to the audio.

Further Note: Below are the annotations plus direct links to the audio performance.

Everett Marcy, Prince Paul Chavchavadze
76. "I Brought Culture to Buffalo in the 90's"

IN PERFORMANCE: MADAME SPIVY
Google Key Words:
Queer Music Heritage Spivy

Madame Spivy
77. "The Alley Cat"

IN PERFORMANCE: MADAME SPIVY
Google Key Words:
Madame Spivy - Queer Music Heritage

Madame Spivy
78. "The Tarantella"

IN PERFORMANCE: MADAME SPIVY
YouTube Key Words:
Madame Spivy – The Tarantella
FULL LYRICS (Scroll down, you'll find them)
https://brianferrarinyc.com/2018/10/30/madames-spivys-tarantella/
Google Key Words:
Madame Spivy's Tarantella Ferrari's Blog

Everett Marcy, Madame Spivy
79. "Why Don't You?"

IN PERFORMANCE: MADAME SPIVY
Google Key Words:
Madame Spivy - Queer Music Heritage

John LaTouche
80. "The Last of the Fleur de Levy"

IN PERFORMANCE: MADAME SPIVY
Google Key Words:
Madame Spivy – Queer Music Heritage

John LaTouche
81. "I Love Town"

IN PERFORMANCE: MADAME SPIVY
Google Key Words:
Madame Spivy – Queer Music Heritage

John LaTouche, Madame Spivy
82. "I Didn't Do a Thing Last Night"

IN PERFORMANCE: MADAME SPIVY
Google Key Words:
Madame Spivy – Queer Music Heritage

Charlotte Kent
83. "The Madame's Lament"

IN PERFORMANCE: MADAME SPIVY
Google Key Words:
Madame Spivy – Queer Music Heritage

Five Sublime Patter Song-and-Dance Men

Just after I sent the final manuscript for this bagatelle to the publisher, I woke one morning and realized I had missed an entire subset of patter songs—those that included dance routines. Five performers came to mind: Fred Astaire, Gene Kelly, Ray Bolger, James Cagney, and Sammy Davis Jr. I knew immediately which numbers should be included in these pages.

But what about the great women singer-dancer-comediennes—Judy Garland, Ginger Rogers, Ruby Keeler, Lady Gaga, Ann Miller, Sutton Foster, Josephine Baker? I screened many a video and found glorious singing and great dancing. But alas, most performances devolved into souped-up, big-and-brassy production numbers—more in keeping with the Super Bowl halftime show than the intimate patter song-and-dance settings of boutique theaters, supper clubs, and living rooms.

ABOUT RAY BOLGER

One evening in April 1956, my father and stepmother took me to the Empire Room of the Waldorf Astoria to see Ray Bolger's nightclub act. In 1939 Bolger became world-famous as the Scarecrow in MGM's The Wizard of Oz.

https://www.youtube.com/watch?v=-hKUh6Kerus

YouTube Key Words:

How Bolger got the scarecrow part

Ray Bolger (1904–87) and his wife, Gwen Rickard, were friends of the family and invited us up to their suite for a drink after the performance.

Etched in my memory are four aspects of the night: (1) The Bolgers were warm, genial, low-key, unassuming folks with a fund of wonderful showbiz memories. (2) Gwen casually mentioned that her tax guy had informed her that afternoon that she had overpaid the IRS $15,000. I was agog! I couldn't imagine people earning so much money that they missed $15,000. My salary as an NBC page was $40 per week (plus an occasional overtime gig). (3) Both Bolgers were in a bit of a swivet because America's most powerful gossip columnist, Walter Winchell—who had started out as a hoofer (as had gangster actor George Raft)—had arrived too late to catch his favorite number, "The Old Soft Shoe." And frankly, "The Old Soft Shoe" laid me out, as it has done every time I have screened it in the ensuing sixty-five years.

A year later, one of my NBC page assignments was a one-hour Sunday variety show, *Washington Square*, starring Ray Bolger. While waiting for the audience to arrive, I sat in the empty theater and watched Bolger rehearse "The Old Soft Shoe" three times, plus I saw the live performance in the show. To me it was (and is) the ultimate patter song-and-dance. I never tire of it.

What follows are three patter song-and-dance numbers interpreted by four truly great performers. (**Note:** "The Babbitt and the Bromide," included here, is the only time Fred Astaire and Gene Kelly performed together.)

Nancy Hamilton (1908–85)
Morgan Lewis (1906–68)
84. "The Old Soft Shoe"

IN PERFORMANCE: RAY BOLGER
https://www.youtube.com/results?search_query=Bolger+Hollywood+Palace+6
YouTube Key Words:
Bolger Hollywood Palace 6

FULL LYRICS:
https://www.musicnotes.com/sheetmusic/mtd.asp?ppn=MN0153456
Google Key Words:
Soft Shoe three to make ready lyrics

Lorenz Hart (1895–1943)
Richard Rogers (1902–79)
I'd Rather Be Right
(From the film *Yankee Doodle Dandy*)
87. "That's Off the Record"

IN PERFORMANCE (as President FDR): JAMES CAGNEY
https://www.youtube.com/watch?v=cmk3qDLVMyE&t=22s
YouTube Key Words:
Cagney's Off the Record 1942
Note: Cagney won the Oscar for best actor.

FULL LYRICS:
https://genius.com/Rodgers-and-hart-off-the-record-lyrics
Google Key Words:
Hart That's Off the Record lyrics

Ira Gershwin (1896–1983)
George Gershwin (1898–1937)
Ziegfeld Follies **(1946 film)**
86. "The Babbitt and the Bromide"

IN PERFORMANCE: FRED ASTAIRE, GENE KELLY
https://www.youtube.com/watch?v=mYVySDLUCy8
YouTube Key Words:
Astaire Kelly Babbitt and Bromide

FULL LYRICS:
https://www.stlyrics.com/lyrics/ziegfeldfollies/thebabbittandthebromide.htm
Google Key Words:
Babbitt and Bromide Lyrics

Jerry Jeff Walker (1942–2020)
87. "Mr. Bojangles"

IN PERFORMANCE: SAMMY DAVIS JR.
https://www.youtube.com/watch?v=-Fju4UajL7g
YouTube Key Words:
Bojangles Sammy Davis

FULL LYRICS:
https://genius.com/Jerry-jeff-walker-mr-bojangles-lyrics
Google Key Words:
Bojangles Lyrics

The Greatest Tap Dance Duet in the History of the World

I don't want to leave you without sharing one final jaw-dropping performance—Fred Astaire and Eleanor Powell's mesmerizing rendition of Cole Porter's "Begin the Beguine" from the MGM musical *Broadway Melody of 1940*. Mirabile dictu, it was done in just two takes! Astaire never made another film with Powell; apparently, he felt she overshadowed him.

https://www.youtube.com/watch?v=0-b4M8jssX8
YouTube Key Words:

Astaire Powell Beguine Tap

A PARTING GIFT

THREE EXTRAORDINARY EVENINGS OF DIALOGUE, MONOLOGUE AND PATTER SONGS

John LaTouche (1914–56) and His Lost Masterpiece

In my short bio of Madame Spivy, I mentioned John LaTouche as one of the lyricists she worked with. LaTouche was a wizard at creating lyrics with delicious rhymes—right up there in the league of Schwenck Gilbert, Noël Coward, and Cole Porter. His masterpiece was *The Golden Apple*. It was not a traditional musical. Rather, it was "sung through"—no spoken dialogue, but rather a series of songs interspersed with recitative, as in traditional opera.

On March 11, 1954, *The Golden Apple* opened at the Phoenix Theater, way off-Broadway at Second Avenue and Twelfth Street, with book and lyrics by John LaTouche and music by Jerome Moross. Moross was a classical, film, and ballet composer who would be nominated for an Academy Award for his score for *The Big Country*.

The show opened to rapturous reviews. My parents immediately ordered tickets. Sixty-seven years later, a number of the scenes are still vivid in my mind. It was the first off-Broadway show to win the Best Musical Award from the New York Drama Critics' Circle. When it moved to Broadway, it ran for a sad 125 performances. It turned out to be a huge hit with reviewers and cognoscenti. But audiences didn't "get it."

I have seen two revivals—in 1962 at the tiny York Theater on Third Avenue and the 2017 City Center "Encores" production. In the latter instance, we had a pre-theater dinner with composer Jerome Moross's daughter, Susanna Moross Tarjan. She regaled us with stories of how "Toosh" and her father had created *The Golden Apple*. In the words of one reviewer of that "Encores" revival:

But oh, the music: 135 glorious minutes of it, unsullied by dialogue. Moross, best known for his film scores to westerns including *The Big Country*, was a member of Aaron Copland's coterie and brings the familiar sound we call American, with its modal harmonies and widely spaced voicings, to a work of astonishing breadth and beauty.

—Jesse Green, *New York Times*, March 11, 2017

In putting together this anthology, I thought a lot about John LaTouche and the tragedy of his life being cut short by a heart attack at age forty-one. Listening to *The Golden Apple* again, I realized it was a series of extraordinary rhyming lyrics—in effect, myriad patter songs interspersed with occasional heart-tugging, gorgeous Broadway melodies and old-fashioned vaudeville song-and-dance numbers (e.g., "Lazy Afternoon," "It's the Going Home Together," "Some Can Be Bought for Money," and "Charybdis and Scylla").

In short, I believe *The Golden Apple* should be in the pantheon of great American musicals along with *Showboat*, *Kiss Me, Kate*, *South Pacific*, and *My Fair Lady*.

May I Share with You *The Golden Apple*?
In prowling the internet—and the wonders of YouTube—I stumbled across a fifty-minute CBS studio-staged production of *The Golden Apple* songs (sans recitative bridges) with Margaret Whiting and Swen Swenson. I loved it. It will supply you with another half dozen patter songs.

PARTING GIFT #1
IN PERFORMANCE; MARGARET WHITING, SWEN SWENSON
https://www.youtube.com/watch?v=j_gj6modjAw&t=187s
YouTube Key Words:
margaret whiting heads a 1977 TV production

FULL LYRICS:
https://archive.org/stream/goldenapplemusic00moro/goldenapplemusic00moro_djvu.txt
Google Key Words:
Full text of the golden apple: a musical in two acts

PARTING GIFT #2
At the Drop of Another Hat
Two deliciously brilliant, zany Brits who toured the British Empire and the U.S. from 1953 to 1967.

IN PERFORMANCE: MICHAEL FLANDERS & DONALD SWANN
https://www.youtube.com/watch?v=OYFiL4p4K9Y&t=2s
YouTube Key Words:
The Only Flanders & Swann Video

PARTING GIFT #3
A fantastic, mesmerizing one-woman (with orchestra) bravura show. Running time: two hours and twenty minutes. All I can say is WOW!
At Liberty
IN PERFORMANCE: ELAINE STRITCH
https://www.youtube.com/watch?v=sNKzYaUzFWs
YouTube Key Words:
Elaine Stritch At Liberty Holly Henderson

Thank you for allowing me this visit with you.
Enjoy!

—DH

P.S. If you have any comments—pro or con—or favorite jokes or patter songs I've missed or a blurb I can use or a complaint, I'd love to hear from you. Give a shout. I'm here.

Denny Hatch
dennyhatch@yahoo.com

ABOUT DENNY HATCH

Denny Hatch has no credentials. He has spent his sixty-year career in advertising, marketing, and direct marketing. He is the author of seven business books and four novels.

Also by Denny (Denison) Hatch

Blog
- *Denny Hatch's Marketing Blog* (2018–)
  It's free. No risk. No obligation. Cancel anytime.
  www.dennyhatch.blogspot.com

Newsletter
- *Who's Mailing What!*
  The monthly analysis and record of the Direct Marketing Archive (1984–2017)

Nonfiction
- *Million Dollar Mailings* (1993, 2001)
- *2,239 Tested Secrets for Direct Marketing Success*, with Don Jackson (1998)
- *Method Marketing: How to Make a Fortune by Getting Inside the Heads of Your Customers* (1999, 2021)
- *Jack Corbett, Mariner* (2002), by A.S. Hatch, edited by and afterword by Denny Hatch
- *Priceline.com: A Layman's Guide to Manipulating the Media* (2003)
- *The Secrets of Emotional, Hot-Button Copywriting* (2010)
- *Career-Changing Takeaways: Quotations, Rules, Aphorisms, Pithy Tips, Quips, Sage Advice, Secrets, Dictums and Truisms in 99 Categories of Marketing, Business and Life* (2010)
- *Write Everything Right!* (2014)

Fiction
- *Cedarhurst Alley: A Lighter-than-Air, Anti-Noise Novel* (1969, 2005)

- *The Fingered City: How the Mafia Marketed a Candidate for Mayor of New York City* (1973, 2016)

- *The Stork: A Comedy about Breeding People* (1976, 2016)

Meet Denny Hatch and See His Twenty-Six-Minute Geezer Fast-Yoga Workout

http://dennyhatch.blogspot.com/2020/03/87-geezer-fast-yoga.html
Google Key Words:
Denny Hatch's Marketing Blog: #87 Geezer Fast-Yoga

Denny Hatch
dennyhatch@yahoo.com

Printed in the United States
by Baker & Taylor Publisher Services